Crosscurrents

Crosscurrents

A World War II Sailor's Voyage Through Life's Stormy Seas to God's Safe Port

By Ray Kerwood

Copyright © 2017 by Ray Kerwood

ISBN: 978-1-5484285-4-9

book and e-book designed and formatted by
ebooklistingservices.com

cover concept by
mclennancreative.com

1 3 5 7 9 10 8 6 4 2
Printed in the United States of America

Dedication

To each of the strong, intelligent, talented, loving, and caring women of my family who have had such a profound positive influence and been such a blessing in my own life:

Grandmother Gentry

Mother Kathleen Kerwood

Wife Donna

Daughter Rebecca Jean

Niece Debbie Miller

Acknowledgements

My most sincere thanks to Jeanette Windle for the final editing of this manuscript. With her professional writing skill and spiritual insight, she has made a reality of my desire to share the story of how God has worked in my life.

My gratitude also to Bill McNamara who has handled all the electronic correspondence needed throughout the entire process.

My thanks to all my Christian friends, lawyers, doctors, pastors, church members, and all those who have encouraged me—they know who they are.

—*Ray Kerwood*

Table of Contents

Crosscurrents

INTRODUCTION

CROSSCURRENTS

A man's heart plans his way, but the Lord directs his steps.

—Proverbs 16:9

I spent most of my World War II service with the Merchant Marines on tanker ships that carried airplane fuel across the ocean. You'll read all about that later. But one trip in particular stands out to me. After the war was over, but before my service was up, I was selected as helmsman for a voyage from Philadelphia, PA, to Jacksonville, FL. My job was to steer the ship into the Jacksonville port.

Although I'd had some experience on prior trips, being helmsman of a loaded tanker is not an easy job. There are crosscurrents. My job coming into port was to turn the steering right or left by rotating the ship's wheel. As I did so, the crosscurrent would take hold, and it was all I could do to offset going too far. This mammoth responsibility left me very uneasy.

Of course, I wasn't completely on my own. The port captain, a resident with comprehensive knowledge of that particular port, was actually in command. He'd boarded the ship once we reached Jacksonville and was directing the action from the ship's bridge, telling me exactly how many degrees right or left I should turn. But I still had to steer her straight. If I miscalculated, I might hit the dock. Hopefully, the port captain would step in before any errors on my end could lead to such a catastrophe.

My life has been somewhat like a helmsman steering a loaded tanker into port. Try as I might to direct the course of my life, there have been other forces at work beyond my control. Just as crosscurrents make for difficulty in steering a ship, so the crosscurrents of my life have carried me in directions I could not have dreamed or imagined. But a Port Captain was present, guiding my actions even before I recognized Him. Rather than sweeping me away into a dangerous situation, the crosscurrents of my life propelled me to a divine Power that has worked through my ordinary existence in ways I cannot otherwise explain.

> Just as crosscurrents make for difficulty in steering a ship, so the crosscurrents of my life have carried me in directions I could not have dreamed or imagined.

Things have happened to me that should not have happened. When I was a boy, I inexplicably avoided injury in a deadly accident. During wartime, I crossed the ocean safely numerous times on ships loaded with flammable fuel while countless other ships were blown up or sunk. I dropped out of college, yet advanced in the oil industry to a position I should not have earned without intervention.

I take none of this for granted. Sometimes I wonder why. Why didn't I die as a boy? Or on a WW2 ship convoy? Why was I given opportunities I shouldn't have been given? I can't answer those questions except that perhaps God has given me, as well as my wife Donna, enormous privilege in order that we in turn might share our lives and resources with others. I'll tell you more about that later, too.

But back to the helm and the loaded tanker I was steering into port. What a relief when we docked safely. I remember the port captain saying to me at the time, "Well done, young man." How appreciative I was of that positive comment. To a young man still in my teens, his words offered comfort that I'd performed well in the difficult duties assigned to me.

I'm no longer a young man. My ninth decade on this earth is now in my rearview mirror. I recently faced a serious health scare, and though my doctor has given me a clean bill of health, I know my ship is closing in on its final port. And I long to hear once again those comforting words I heard at a Jacksonville ship dock. But this time from the Port Captain who has been keeping my ship on its course all these years and is now guiding me into safe harbor: "Well done, Ray Kerwood, good and faithful servant."

These are my stories, yes. But this is not a story about how wonderful Ray Kerwood is. It is a story about how faithful God has been. About how God has worked and how He is working through ordinary lives in extraordinary ways. Not just my life, but so many others you will meet in the following pages. It is my wish that you share these stories with your friends, your neighbors, people you know who may need a closer acquaintance with a God who is faithful, loving, and good. Don't tell them what a great guy Ray Kerwood is. Tell them what a great God Ray Kerwood serves.

That is all I care to leave behind—a record of God's goodness in my life and an invitation to you to let God guide you safely into port. When I was in the Merchant Marines, we faced our share of troubles on the sea. We weren't spared storms or threats of attack. Life offers no such promises either. God has been good to me, yes. But you'll see that it hasn't always been easy. God has led me through calm waters, but also through stormy tempests I never thought to survive. Not to mention that I am far from a perfect human being. I've made mistakes. I have regrets.

But through storm and calm, God's presence in my life has been unmistakable. It is my prayer that you will see His presence in your life, too. And if you haven't done so already, that you will take those first steps toward believing our Port Captain is a God of extraordinary power, extraordinary grace, and extraordinary love, who wants you to be His.

CHAPTER ONE

WHAT HAPPENS IN VEGAS

And in Your book they all were written, the days fashioned for me, when as yet there were none of them.

—Psalm 139:16

Las Vegas. Sin City. What happens there stays there, so they say. But I'll never forget what happened to me there. Or didn't happen, as it turned out.

Born in Logan, West Virginia, on January 27, 1926, I was named after my father, Ray W. Kerwood, though my middle name is Kenna to distinguish between the two of us. My father was a mechanic by trade, operating his own tire and automobile repair shop. My mother, Kathleen K. Kerwood, was a school teacher, though she'd given that up when she married at age nineteen. If nineteen seems young today for teaching school, it was not uncommon then to graduate from school by age sixteen, study for a teaching certificate, then teach in a one-room rural schoolhouse before marriage, college, or another profession.

In 1928, two years after my own birth, my younger sister Nancy was born. As far as I remember, our childhood ran smoothly enough until 1932, when my father was diagnosed with advanced tuberculosis, which left him too physically weak to continue his repair-shop business. There was no effective cure for tuberculosis in those days, but a common treatment was sending TB patients to a hot, dry climate, believed to be easier on their laboring lungs. Which is how we ended up leaving Logan, WV, for the desert habitat of Las Vegas, Nevada.

✝

My father went ahead to Las Vegas on his own to find housing. It was six months before he arranged for the rest of us to join him. This was the era of the Great Depression, and Nevada might as well have been on another planet. But my mother loaded my sister Nancy and me into an old, beat-up Ford and began driving. Friends of my mother, another teacher and her brother, followed us in their own vehicle in case we broke down. They must have held my mother in very high regard, as the gas expenditure alone would have been a serious financial sacrifice for them.

It took seven long days to cover the 2100+ miles from Logan to Las Vegas. We had little money for gas, repairs, or food, much less to stay in motels along the way. So we spent nights sleeping in the car on the side of the road or at rest areas along the way. I have little memory of that trip.

We arrived in Las Vegas to find a small, two-room adobe house waiting for us on the very edge of town surrounded by arid desert. Las Vegas at that time was on the cusp of a population boom, unrecognizable as the city its residents know today. Our neighborhood was simply scattered houses bordering the main road that headed out of town into the desert. We had no close neighbors. Neither did we have running water or electricity. Two kerosene lamps provided light. My parents rigged up a refrigeration system, which was just a crate covered by a wet cloth with water running over it to keep cool any food inside.

By this time, I was six years old, my sister four. Even before my father's illness, I don't remember having a close relationship with him. He was not a kind, loving man, either to his children or his wife. One stark memory when we first arrived in Las Vegas illustrates what would be a pattern for our relationship. I hadn't seen my father for six months and was excited to see him. The car window where I sat was rolled down, so I stuck my head out to greet him.

Unfortunately, he had leaned in to look through the window at the same moment, so we ended up butting heads. Instead of treating it as the minor accident it was, he glared down at me and said angrily, as though I'd been deliberately naughty, "Ray Kenna, you've started already!"

> Unfortunately, he had leaned in to look through the window at the same moment, so we ended up butting heads.

That was the only greeting I received from my father. My only other memories of him involve him telling an off-colored joke and his constant coughing around Nancy and me. He made no attempt to cover his mouth or keep his disease-riddled sputum from landing on us. Sometimes it seemed he was deliberately coughing in our faces, as though he either wanted to infect us or just didn't care. When my mother begged him not to cough in our presence, he would turn on her with verbal abuse.

My mother was such a contrast to my father. Morning, noon, and night, she waited on him. During the constant hacking and sleepless nights, she demonstrated unfailing love and never lost patience with my father, though he, in contrast, was both unloving and verbally abusive. She did her best as well to keep us away from him, especially when he was coughing, and to shield us from his verbal abuse as well as his illness.

Years later when I was in high school, I'd been digging around in a drawer, looking for something else, when I found a letter my father had written to my mother after he entered a sanitarium. It was the vilest thing I had ever read, accusing her of infidelity. He had no excuse for doing such a nasty thing. Yet to my knowledge, my mother never criticized him. When I mentioned his actions to her after his death, she replied, "Ray, honey, he was sick and couldn't help it." It still brings me to tears when I think about how she cared for him.

With my father too sick to work and my mother having to remain home to care for him and two children, our income was practically nothing. Both sets of grandparents had been left behind in West Virginia. My paternal grandparents operated a small restaurant there. But the Great Depression had driven them into bankruptcy, so they couldn't offer any help. My maternal grandfather, John Kenna Gentry, was a mine-safety inspector, but he was also a heavy drinker and struggled holding onto any job for long.

Still, he and my grandmother did send meager sums of money as they could. How we ate, I really don't remember, especially once my younger brother Jim was born, adding another mouth to feed. I do remember receiving food at least once from the local Red Cross. But our makeshift "refrigerator" stayed mostly empty.

Among my few positive memories of Las Vegas were several boys from nearby homes who became my playmates. But this led to the worst experience of my short life to that point. One of our favorite playtime activities was burrowing in a nearby sand dune. My friends and I had cleared a passageway about fifteen feet in length, and on each side of the passageway, we dug out a space with enough room to lie down and take a nap. For several days in succession, we crawled in there to play and nap. Each time, this necessitated clearing out the sand that had accumulated in our absence.

Then one day, two of the boys stopped by to ask if I'd like to come along to the sand dune. For some reason, of which I have no recollection today, I told them I wasn't able to go with them, but they could catch me the next day. About mid-afternoon, I heard ambulances race past our house, sirens wailing loudly. They were headed to the sand dune. The tunnel we'd dug had caved in, trapping my friends inside. The rescue squad was unable to reach them before they'd suffocated.

> The tunnel we'd dug had caved in, trapping my friends inside. The rescue squad was unable to reach them before they'd suffocated.

All these years later, that memory still haunts me. I could have been with them. On any other day, I would have been. How narrowly I'd escaped death! And why me instead of my friends?

One other less unhappy memory remains of our time in Nevada. Not long before we left to move back to West Virginia, some friends drove us to see Hoover Dam, still in the process of construction at that time. They say Hoover Dam is one of the seven modern engineering wonders of the United States. I can believe it. The site was a beehive of activity with a procession of trucks ferrying in construction materials to that part of the dam currently being built. I surveyed this tremendous feat of engineering with awe, marveling at such a phenomenal undertaking.

I remember also seeing hundreds of small structures that housed thousands of workers who'd come from all over the country to work on the dam. Those structures would eventually become Boulder City. Even though the dam wouldn't be finished for several years and was just beginning to take shape, its sheer grandeur and scope made an indelible impression on my young mind.

But of course, we'd moved to Las Vegas solely on account of my father's illness. After a year and a half there, his health showed no improvement. In fact, despite my mother's selfless nursing, he grew progressively worse to the point that the doctors recommended he enter a sanitarium specializing in the treatment of tuberculosis. Since there was no benefit to remaining any longer in Las Vegas, my parents decided to find a sanitarium back east closer to family.

One was recommended to them in the town of Beckley, WV, just sixty miles from where my mother's parents lived in Charleston, WV, so my mother, siblings, and I moved in with them while my father entered the sanitarium. Grandfather and Grandmother Gentry still had two of their own children at home, my uncle John (named after his father) and my aunt Caroline, which meant there were eight people living in one small third-floor apartment.

Less than a year later, my father died at the age of just thirty-two. I was nine or ten at the time, but I felt no real emotion at his death. Except those months in Las Vegas when he was actively unkind and uncaring, my father had been a non-entity throughout my childhood life. Once he was in the sanitarium, I don't remember ever even visiting him. So if I felt some shock and surprise at his death, I definitely felt no grief.

> Less than a year later,
> my father died at the
> age of just thirty-two.

I do remember asking my mother, "Will you get remarried again?"

I don't remember her response, but she never did remarry while she was raising my siblings and me. She eventually did remarry in 1964, after we were all adults, only three years before she in turn died of cancer.

I have never been back to Nevada, but I will never forget my short time there, above all because of what happened to my friends. I will never know just why I was spared that day and they weren't. But what has become clear to me is that God uses ordinary people to carry out His extraordinary plan. He had something in mind for my life that did not involve it ending on that day, even though it would take me a lifetime to see it.

What I did know was this. My friends had died. I had lived. It would be many years before I truly understood how death could lead to life.

CHAPTER TWO

IN THE BLINK OF AN EYE

You do not know what will happen tomorrow. For
what is your life? It is even a vapor that appears for
a little time and then vanishes away.

—James 4:14

I was fifteen years old when the world changed in a single
moment. The day was December 7, 1941. I still remember
sitting at the time with my uncle John in the Kearse
movie theater in Charleston, WV. Back then, the theaters
played news reels before the main attraction instead of
commercials or movie trailers like they do now. I was
impatiently waiting for the news to finish so we could watch
the movie when suddenly an attack on the American naval
base at Pearl Harbor in Hawaii flashed on the screen. No one
had any interest in the movie after that! Even at age fifteen,
I knew this was the end of a normal teenage life.

By that point, my mother, brother Jim, sister Nancy, and
I had settled into life with my grandparents. Grandmother
Gentry was a truly remarkable woman, somehow managing
to keep eight household members fed on just $2 a day. My
mother too taught me by example the value of hard work.
Once he became ill, my father had never again been able to

provide for our family financially. So once we returned from Las Vegas, my mother took a job with the state of West Virginia in the education department, for which she earned $70 a month. She held that job for at least thirty years after my father died.

I remember one year when my mother received a promotion and the *Charleston Gazette* wrote an article covering the honor. Here is how the news reporter described her:

> Kathleen Gentry Kerwood was perpetually pleasant as a statistician for the Board of School Finance, [and] has the same disposition after her promotion to senior statistical clerk for the State Department of Education. She is a rare person who can deal with cold facts and figures while constantly manifesting a warm personality.

Years later, I met United States Senator Robert C. Byrd of West Virginia, who had dealt with my mother on various projects, including providing him with numerous calculations about education finances for the state. Senator Byrd had nothing but kind things to say about my mother. He told me she'd often worked overtime and weekends to accommodate his requests. Her example of hard work and dedication became one I have endeavored to follow all my life.

Grandfather Gentry provided somewhat of a father figure for all us kids, including teaching us good manners. But he was dealing with his own drinking issues and bad health, so he was not a major influence in our lives. In truth, I grew up without any real father figure. But what I did have was a succession of strong, intelligent, hard-working, caring women—Grandmother Gentry, my mother, my wife Donna, my daughter Rebecca—who have all been a great influence and blessing in my own life. And ultimately, I came to know what it meant to have a father when I met my true heavenly Father.

My uncle John was just two years older than me, so we grew up more like brothers than uncle and nephew. We attended school together, first at Kanawha Grade School, then Thomas Jefferson Junior High. Though we were two grades apart, we hung out with the same friends and enjoyed the same activities, such as learning how to play poker, participating in sporting activities, and going to the local movie theater, which was just five cents before noon and a dime in the afternoon. By the time we were in high school, we considered ourselves quite the ladies' men and were both dating regularly.

> That all changed
> with Pearl Harbor.

That all changed with Pearl Harbor. Over the next six months, it became apparent the government would be drafting soldiers for the Armed Forces. By the time I reached the eleventh grade a year later, the draft was well underway. Those boys in their senior year of high school began disappearing from class. My uncle John entered the U.S. Navy Air Corp as soon as he turned eighteen. He graduated as a pilot and later participated in the first air strike over Japan. He eventually received the Distinguished Flying Cross as well as the Medal of Honor with three oak leaf clusters.

Shortly after the war at just twenty-four years of age, John died of leukemia. That's an unusual cause of death for someone who was always a healthy, athletic young man. With all that emerged later of atom bombs and the effects of radiation, we had to wonder if his illness was related to his military service in the Japanese theater of war, but we never found out if there was any connection.

I was determined to do my own part for the war, but at fifteen I couldn't enlist. Instead, I poured my energy into athletics, participating in basketball, football and track. By eleventh grade, I was playing first string and received accolades in every sport I participated in. I was elected captain of the track team. In my junior year, I ran the hundred-yard dash in 10.3 seconds and the quarter-mile in 52.2 seconds, which was only three-tenths of a second off the state record that had stood for twenty years.

I was also always looking for a job to earn money. With eight people living on such tight finances, we kids—my sister Nancy, my brother Jim, my uncle John, my aunt Caroline, and me—understood from a very early age that we were expected to find work as soon as we were able. In fact, I was only thirteen when I landed my first job at Bohnert's Flower Shop in Charleston, WV.

The year was 1939, well before my uncle John had left to fight. It was the Easter season, during which time the shop employed children to assemble corsages for twenty cents an hour. John and I worked the night shift, and halfway through one shift around midnight, I sat down. I had been working dutifully until then, but the supervisor happened to be walking by. When she spotted me sitting, she reacted angrily. "Hey there, he's sitting down!"

My uncle John was quick to defend me. "His hands are moving, ain't they?"

From then on, I'd always held some kind of job. During each summer, I worked at different seasonal jobs. One summer, I poured concrete, laying sidewalks at various schools in the county. The summer before eleventh grade, I found work through an unemployment agency at a refrigeration company. In those days, refrigeration units were like an entire room in a house. A crew of three men plus the owner of the company, Mr. Thrush, would assemble the enclosure, lifting the sides up and molding them together, then install the refrigeration system.

The job didn't pay much, and the heavy work required a set of strong muscles. But it taught me to work together as a team. At the end of that summer, Mr. Thrush offered to bring me on permanently. When I told him I was still in high school, he was surprised. I looked older than I was, and I guess my work ethic revealed some maturity.

> The job didn't pay much, and the heavy work required a set of strong muscles. But it taught me to work together as a team.

The summer before my senior year, my football coach at Charleston High School, Lyle Rich, got me a job running the three tennis courts located at Laidley Field. This was a downtown Charleston sports complex where our high school football team had often played games. Along with coaching high school football, Lyle Rich worked in various capacities at Laidley Field. That summer he was going out of state to visit family, so he needed a substitute to put up the nets every day for the tennis courts and handle customers and sales. The courts rented for thirty-five cents an hour, while Cokes went for a nickel. My agreement with the coach was to send him fifty percent of anything I made from rental fees.

This proved the beginning of my training in business management as I met people and learned how to please customers. At the end of each day, I would return to our sweltering apartment (no air-conditioning then!), and my mother and I would count all the cash I had collected. Every month all summer long, I faithfully sent half to my coach. One time when I could not account for $4, I even ended up taking the loss from my own pocket. Coach Rich later told me I was the first student he'd hired who had fulfilled the agreement. From my perspective, I saw it as an opportunity to make some spending money, but also to gain an unusual degree of business experience for my young age.

At this time in my life, I would not have called myself spiritual, but neither was I an atheist. I did my best to be honest and moral and hardworking. I treated girls with respect. Just once when I was twelve years old, I remember being out in the middle of a corn field when I chose to use God's name in vain. I felt so immediately guilty that I knelt down right there in the corn field to ask forgiveness. That was the last time I remember ever taking the Lord's name in vain.

I also occasionally attended an Episcopalian church, and somewhere I'd acquired a necklace with a little cross I wore at school. Something about that cross and my conduct must have led my coaches to believe I was a God-fearing young man, because I can remember my basketball coach, Eddie King, asking me to lead in prayer before a game. I don't remember ever reading a Bible then. But I owned a Book of Common Prayer, which was part of the Episcopalian liturgy, which I read from time to time and even took with me when I left home. If I thought about religion and faith, it was superficially. But I did take pride in having a strong moral code and work ethic.

> Something about that cross and my conduct must have led my coaches to believe I was a God-fearing young man.

Of course, all these activities were putting in time until I could legally join up to fight the Nazis. By the time I turned eighteen, the United States was entering its third year of war. I was now in my senior year of high school, and I knew I wouldn't graduate without being drafted, so I decided to volunteer. At least that way I'd have some control over where I ended up.

I'd heard about the Merchant Marine Academy from a football buddy. They trained officers for the Merchant Marine, which in WW2 became the largest sealift in human history, ferrying troops, supplies, ammo, fuel, and every other item needed to run a war across the Atlantic and in the Pacific. At that time, I had no idea that the Merchant Marine also had the highest casualty rate in the Allied Forces. What attracted me was that the training program was only three months on land before being assigned to a ship for continued training. Since I wanted to get overseas as quickly as possible, it seemed a perfect fit.

As soon as I'd turned eighteen, I signed up for Officers Candidate School at the Kings Point Merchant Marine Academy in New York. I was accepted, and in April, 1944, I entered the Academy as a cadet midshipman. Normally, I wouldn't have received my high school diploma until May. But it was customary then to allow early graduation to students who were heading to war, so the school just winked at those last thirty days.

Part of the initial three-month training program at the Academy included practical experience aboard a sailing ship in New York Harbor. I had graduated high school with excellent grades, but during my training, I failed the navigation portion of studies. I went before a review board to determine if I could continue. Fortunately, one of the officers on the board took an interest in me and intervened to give me a second opportunity. My failure had been a wake-up call that certainly got my attention. From that point on, I applied myself diligently to my studies and completed the course with a passing grade.

CHAPTER THREE

STORMY SEAS

.●●..●●..●●..●●.

God is our refuge and strength, a very present help
in trouble. Therefore, we will not fear . . . though
the mountains be carried into the midst of the sea;
though its waters roar and be troubled.

—Psalm 46:1-3

It had been a close call whether I went to sea or flunked
out. But just three months after entering the Academy,
on July 3, 1944, I'd achieved my ambition and now found
myself on a ship heading overseas to serve my country
against its enemies. During my service, I sailed on two kinds
of ships—a Liberty ship and a T-2 tanker. Liberty ships
carried bulk cargo, while tankers hauled liquids such as fuel.
At the beginning of the war, it took six months to build and
launch the first Liberty ship. By the end of the war, American
shipyards were putting out a Liberty ship in seven days.

My first assignment was to the S.S. William Wirt, a Liberty
ship owned by Alcoa Aluminum Company, which was sailing
to Dutch Guiana (now Suriname) to pick up a load of bauxite
ore, necessary for the production of aluminum. That first trip

was my introduction to all aspects of becoming a deck officer in the Merchant Marines. We reached Dutch Guiana without

incident, where we picked up the bauxite. On our return trip, we were traveling in the company of three other Liberty ships when we neared Cape Hatteras off the coast of North Carolina.

During the night, a severe storm arose. The ships were under total night blackout during this time, meaning that no lights were permitted that could give away our position to enemy submarines or aircraft. Because of this, we couldn't see each other's position. In the morning, we received a report that one of the other ships had sunk. It appeared that hatches had been left open, allowing the storm's high waves to flood the ship. Whether this was through the captain's neglect, or someone else was responsible for the open hatches, the whole ship had been lost.

> In the morning, we received a report that one of the other ships had sunk. It appeared that hatches had been left open, allowing the storm's high waves to flood the ship.

A few sailors survived on one of the lifeboats. Our own ship reached Philadelphia safely and discharged our cargo of bauxite. Young men can feel pretty invincible about their own mortality, and I didn't really think much about the chances of my own death or what would happen if I died. But as with that sand tunnel in my childhood, I was certainly sobered at the reflection that I had been spared while others died.

That event was not the last time my own mortality was brought sharply home to me. One of my responsibilities while in port waiting for our next voyage was learning how to use the huge cargo winch for loading freight. On one particular day, I was helping load cargo when another ship passed by us unusually fast. Even at sea, this was poor seamanship. But in port, as we were at the time, it was careless and dangerous, resulting in a large swell that sharply rocked our ship.

At that moment, I was holding a cable with my right hand. The swell caused the cable to be yanked through a cast-iron turnbuckle. We wore gloves to protect our hands while loading, and the sudden jerking of the cable pulled my right glove into the turnbuckle. Thankfully, I managed to snatch my hand free just in time. It was sore for a week or two, but I didn't mind, since if I hadn't been able to pull free, my arm would have been severed up to my shoulder. I might not have been doing much praying at that point, but my occasional church visits had been enough for me to recognize immediately that God had protected me. Right then I paused to thank God for His deliverance.

After another successful trip to pick up a load of bauxite ore, I boarded a T-2 tanker, the S.S. Cross Keys, owned by Gulf Oil Corporation. Little did I know how influential that company name would become in my life just ten years later. All told, I made five round-trip voyages across the Atlantic on this vessel. Four of these were to deliver our cargo, six million gallons of aviation gas, to English ports such as Bristol, Avonmouth, and the straits of Dover, as well as to Algiers in North Africa. On three voyages, we carried as well a deck cargo of seventeen airplanes, a mixture of P-38 and P-51 fighter planes.

**S.S. CROSS KEYS
1946**

As you might imagine, the tankers we sailed on were extremely vulnerable because of our flammable cargo. Should we be struck by a torpedo, the ship would explode, sinking within minutes. The strike didn't even need to be on a strategic part of the craft. So long as the torpedo hit the ship, flames from the ignited fuel would envelop the ship, turning the iron decks into a blistering inferno. All of which made escape for the forty men onboard unlikely. In contrast, a cargo ship would linger longer before sinking and might even survive if hit in the stern or bow.

I remember well that first day as all thirty-eight crew members assembled on deck while our stern-faced captain addressed us: "Men, I am your captain. And under the Articles of War, I have complete and full life and death authority. So I'll make it short and sweet. Our mission is to deliver this aviation gas safely because our planes need it desperately, and if humanly possible, we're going to do it. But I want you to hear this good. I don't make it a habit of asking twice for anyone to do anything. Do I make myself clear?"

I not only heard him, but if the captain had ordered, "Overboard!", I wouldn't have paused to ask which side.

My first voyage on the S.S. Cross Keys took us to Bristol, England, and safely back to Gulf Oil's Philadelphia Girard Point Refinery, despite reports of several U-boats roaming the north Atlantic during our trip. During that first tanker voyage, I was privileged to be assigned as "gopher" to all three of the ship's deck officers—i.e., the chief mate, second mate, and third mate. This was part of my continued on-ship officer training, exposing me to every aspect of becoming a third officer.

We left Philadelphia for our second voyage on November 18, 1944. I was almost nineteen years old by this point and still somewhat of a tenderfoot. On our second day at sea, I was standing watch with the second mate on the bridge when the torpedo detector sounded. We had just twenty-five seconds to avert a hit. The second mate was a diminutive man, a good foot shorter than my own height of six-foot-four and no more than one hundred-forty pounds soaking wet with what I considered a rather effeminate voice. But I learned in the next moments that intestinal fortitude comes in all shapes and sizes. He informed me that we needed to pick up the torpedo's wake to know which way to turn the ship in order to avoid impact. He had been torpedoed once and did not want to experience that again. Seconds later, he spotted the wake.

> He informed me that we needed to pick up the torpedo's wake to know which way to turn the ship in order to avoid impact.

"Hard starboard!" he shouted to the helmsman. The helmsman turned the ship sharply right, taking us out of the torpedo's path. We stood and watched as potential disaster passed us by. Many lives had just been saved by the second mate's quick action. I learned a couple lessons that day. One, not to judge by appearance. And once again, that life can be fragile and fleeting.

At the beginning of World War II, American ships typically sailed individually. But by the end of 1942, thousands of Allied ships had been sunk by enemy fire, 175 ships in just one month. So the War Shipping Administration began organizing transatlantic convoys of thirty-five to a hundred ships, guarded by an outer perimeter of U.S. Navy destroyers. The commodore in command of the convoy would travel on the lead ship.

On another of my voyages, we were part of one such convoy crossing the North Atlantic during a terrible storm.

Towards dusk, I was on the bridge (the ship's wheelhouse from which the captain commanded the ship) when the captain spotted a lifeboat coming loose. He instructed me to call for an able-bodied sailor to secure the lifeboat.

"Captain, I can do that," I responded.

He hesitated a little, since that wasn't a bridge officer's job. But he said okay, so I went outside. During such storms, the ship would rise up out of the water as the waves passed under it, then slam back down. If a wave hit you, it could toss you around like a pebble. Still, I managed to reach the life boat. It took me fifteen to twenty minutes to tie it down securely.

I was heading back to the bridge when an enormous wave swept over the deck, slamming me into a guard rail. I was nearly knocked unconscious. The railing consisted of metal bars a good eighteen inches apart with open space in between. As I regained my bearings, I realized that one of my arms was caught backward over a crossbar, which had kept me from being swept out through the open bars. Other than God's providence, there was no explanation as to why I had not been tossed into the north Atlantic. Under such circumstances, there would have been no effort to recover a man overboard. They would simply report it later. Once again, superficial Christian though I was at the time, I poured out my gratitude to God for sparing my life.

On another convoy run, March 21, 1945, we had almost reached England when the S.S. Cross Keys fell behind the rest of convoy, which was mostly C3 cargo ships. The commodore commanding the convoy was maintaining a speed of 19-21 knots, while the normal top speed of the S.S. Cross Keys was only 17-18 knots. We just couldn't maintain the convoy's speed. As we fell increasingly behind, we received a communication from the commodore's ship that German submarines were lurking near the convoy. If we didn't close the gap, we'd be an easy target.

The captain took this seriously since another convoy ship carrying ammunition just a half-mile from our position had been blown out of the water the night before, lighting up the night sky for several minutes like a fireworks display. I was in the wheelhouse when the captain called through the intercom to Red, the chief engineer, to increase the engines' RPMs (revolutions per minute). This in turn would increase our speed.

"Captain, all the gauges down here are in the extreme danger zone," Red called back. "Any further increase in speed will result in the engines being shut down permanently by exploding!"

The captain was not happy. But he waited another five minutes, during which we fell even further behind. Then he called the engine room again. This time he shouted furiously, "Red, you SOB, increase ship speed sufficient to catch up to the convoy!"

> He waited another five minutes, during which we fell even further behind.

Actually, his words were a little less polite than that! Red reluctantly complied. The gauge readings now indicated imminent danger for the engines. Certainly, there was no reason they didn't explode. But somehow they held together, and we were able to catch up to the convoy. Another indication of God's providence, since if the engines hadn't held, our T-2 tanker would have been another ship casualty. Or we might instead have been sunk by a German torpedo, leaving few or no survivors.

The next day, Red apologized to the captain for his foot-dragging. The captain just shrugged it off, saying, "Well, you got 'em, didn't you?" Red was certainly one outstanding engineer to coax those engines safely into port, and the captain knew that.

One other incident during my time in the Merchant Marines always stuck in my mind. We'd been at sea with no land in sight for thirteen days before our ship headed back to New York harbor. I was on duty with the captain on the bridge when the captain commented that we should be catching sight shortly of Ambrose Light. This was the light station that marked the entrance into the port of New York.

Not sixty seconds after the captain made that comment, I spotted the bright beacon of Ambrose Light on the horizon. In my day, it was actually an anchored light ship, in essence, a floating lighthouse, though in the sixties a tower was built to replace the ship. Little though I was thinking about God in those days, it struck me how precisely God had designed this universe, above all, the stars in the heavens, that a ship captain could navigate so accurately as to know within a sixty-second time frame exactly where he was on this planet.

World War II ended with Germany's surrender on May 8, 1945, though fighting continued in the Pacific for several more months until Japan surrendered September 2, 1945. It took several months after Germany's surrender before I received my honorable discharge from the Merchant Marines in August, 1945.

By the end of the war, the percentage of war-related deaths in the Merchant Marines would prove to be the highest of any military service, including the Marines, although our living conditions aboard ship were perhaps no comparison to the hardship of Marine combat. In total, one out of every twenty-six mariners serving aboard merchant ships during World War II died in the line of duty. One main factor in the casualty rate was the number of convoy ships sunk by German torpedoes and the icy storms of the North Atlantic.

Just recently, I was watching a program on the History Channel about the *USS Indianapolis*, a carrier that was torpedoed by the Japanese in 1945. The ship sank in just twelve minutes. Those men who survived the ship's sinking were stranded in the water for four days. They endured lack of food, lack of water, saltwater poisoning, and shark attacks.

Watching this television program deeply affected my emotions. I couldn't help, but think back to my crossings of the Atlantic Ocean, carrying sufficient high-octane explosive fuel to set the ocean aflame. The suffering of these sailors could so easily have ended up being my own story.

CHAPTER FOUR

DONNA

He who finds a wife finds a good thing, and obtains
favor from the Lord.

—Proverbs 18:22

After my honorable discharge, I continued to work with
the Merchant Marines for another year to earn money
while I made up my mind just where I wanted to
attend college. I made several more voyages, on one of them
serving as acting third mate, on others just as an able-bodied
seaman. If just as much hard work, at least that final year
as a sailor after the war ended was far less hazardous than
my earlier danger-filled experiences.

I ended up receiving athletic scholarship offers from
several different colleges—University of Tennessee, North
Carolina University, Georgia Tech, Virginia Polytechnic
Institute, and the University of Miami. Virginia Polytechnic
Institute in Blacksburg, Virginia, was an excellent
engineering school and close to home, so I chose to attend
there, which I did on a football scholarship.

With my service experience and officer training, plus a
partial year of college, I should have graduated from VPI in
just two-and-a-half years. But that didn't happen. I was

taking a full load of engineering classes and practicing football twice a day, which left me feeling quite overwhelmed. Then that summer after my first year at VPI, I took a job working for my maternal grandfather, John Kenna Gentry.

> I was taking a full load of engineering classes and practicing football twice a day, which left me feeling quite overwhelmed.

By this time, Grandfather Gentry was no longer a mine safety inspector with the state of WV, but a coal mine owner in his own right. All those years he'd spent inspecting mines from a safety viewpoint had made him an expert in the business. His problems with alcohol had left him sickly and cost him a number of jobs. So when some friends in the coal industry suggested they go into partnership, finding and mining their own coal leases in the Rainelle area of Greenbrier County, WV, he'd agreed. The result was Rainelle Coal Company.

Grandfather Gentry eventually bought out his partners. RCC was a strip mine enterprise, which meant mining coal on the surface vs. underground shafts. The process for such a mine involved paying people to core drill on possible property leases, looking for coal seams. By the time I was in college, one of these core drills had located a seam of pure coal about fifty inches deep in vertical thickness. In the coal industry, this was like pure gold, a fortune for whoever held the mining lease.

Which ended up being Grandfather Gentry. My first job for him that summer was cleaning coal. At the time, I thought this would just be a short-term summer job. But later that same summer, I met the wonderful woman to whom I have now been married for more than seventy years, and I never did return to college.

> Later that same summer, I met the wonderful woman to whom I have now been married for more than seventy years.

I actually met Donna through my friend Dave. He'd been pestering me to go on a double date with him, his steady girlfriend Ruby, and her friend Margie. I turned him down twice, telling him I wasn't interested, especially since they lived back in Charleston, and I was working for the summer eighty miles away at the Rainelle coal mine. But he was so insistent, I finally relented and went on the date. Dave and I met up with Margie and Ruby, and we all went out together to Camden Park, a twenty-six acre amusement park with a carousel, roller-coaster, and other attractions near Huntington, West Virginia. Margie was nice. I was nice. But there was no real spark.

When we returned from the park, we all went to Margie's house, and she invited us in. I was sitting in the living room when a vision of beauty emerged from the kitchen and walked past me. The vision was Margie's sister Donna, and it was love at first sight. At least for me! As she floated past me, I could hear the lyrics of the song "To Each His Own". Whether it was playing on the radio or in my fantasy, I can't be sure. I simply said to myself, "That's for me!"

Donna and I got to chatting, which left me even more taken with Margie's sister. Once Dave and I left the house, I asked him for Donna's telephone number. I later learned that after our visit, she had asked Margie, "Which one are you dating?"

"The long, lanky one," Margie told her.

In actuality, I never did date Margie except that one arranged double-date. She was cute, but too much of an extrovert for my taste. Donna was more serious-minded, and so was I, which immediately struck a chord between us. Dave did give me Donna's number, and I immediately called to ask her for a date. During the next several months, I no longer found the eighty miles between Rainelle and Charleston too long of a drive. I would head down to see Donna at least every other week. I also met the rest of her family, including her father Lester, mother Alma, and her brother Jim.

Lester was not impressed with me at all. He was an overbearing, egocentric man who thought no one but him had a lick of sense. It wasn't long before I realized that Donna didn't have a very happy home life. Lester always treated Donna as though she were less competent than her effervescent older sister. A good example was that he taught Margie to drive when she turned sixteen. But when Donna turned sixteen a couple years later, he told her she wasn't capable of learning and refused to teach her.

He didn't think Donna was capable of college studies either, so Donna paid her own way through secretarial school. He also told her she'd never do better than working at the five-and-dime store. But by the time I met her, she was working as the private secretary for the owner of Kuhn Construction Company in Charleston. She was beautiful, smart, hard-working, interesting to talk to, and I couldn't believe my good fortune that she'd fall in love with someone like me. But her father had done such a number on her self-confidence and self-esteem, I always had to encourage her not to sell herself short just because her father didn't have the good sense to appreciate what a special daughter he'd been given.

I in turn didn't allow Donna's father to intimidate me at all. I didn't even bother getting his permission before asking Donna to marry me. When he found out, he just grunted at me, "So I guess you all are going through with this thing!"

"Yes, we are," I replied shortly.

And that was that! If he'd actually cared about Donna, he might have made more of a fuss. But in fact, he treated both daughters as though he wanted to get rid of them and was happy to marry them off to get them out of the house.

Donna and I were married on November 27, 1947. We were both 21 years old. Back then, the bride's parents were usually expected to cover the wedding costs. Donna's father offered no help at all, but Donna had a good job and was able to cover the wedding costs on her own. Of course, our wedding costs were nothing like weddings today. $10 for the cake. $15 for the organist. Big spender that I am, I paid a whopping $25 for the preacher. Donna's parents did host the reception in their home with coffee and tea for refreshments.

Ray and Donna's Wedding—November 27, 1947

I quit college and continued working for my grandfather at the Rainelle coal mine. Since this was eighty miles from Charleston, Donna quit her job too, and we moved to a rustic one-room cabin in the mountains near Rainelle. I was working as a common laborer, cleaning coal for $1.63 an hour, so money was tight.

> We moved to a rustic one-room cabin in the mountains near Rainelle.

Then, just a few months after Donna and I were married, my grandfather discovered that two of his overseers, the Huff brothers, were stealing from the company. In the late 1940s, Rainelle Coal Company was producing a thousand tons of coal a day, the equivalent of about fifteen railroad cars. The coal would then be transported to Tidewater, VA, primarily for export overseas. The brothers were joint superintendents, one supervising the day shift, the other supervising the night shift. But a company audit revealed that they'd been selling a considerable amount of the mined coal on the side and pocketing the monies.

Though I was only twenty-two years old, Grandfather Gentry gave me the responsibility of taking over the entire project as superintendent, both day and night shift. I was aware that this promotion was temporary, maybe sixty to ninety days until my grandfather could hire a qualified superintendent. But with a wife to support, I was more than happy to earn a superintendent's salary of $500 a month plus a car and expenses. This was less generous than it sounds, considering my grandfather had been paying the Huff brothers a total of $3000.00 a month along with a commission agreement.

Unfortunately, the superintendent job turned out to be seventy hours a week, which meant the hourly wage worked out to $1.66 an hour. When I was a common laborer, workers' rights regulations stipulated I could work only eight hours a day, so while I might be making more money now, by the hour it worked out to just three cents an hour increase in my wages. Still, it was better money overall, and I didn't mind hard work. My "short-term" position went on for two full years. I guess Grandfather Gentry decided that the large sum of money he'd have to shell out to bring in an experienced mine superintendent wasn't worth the bargain he was getting in me!

Fortunately for me, both the day and night shifts had excellent, highly experienced foremen. And though I was young, I'd been the "man of the house", so to speak, early in my life. Military service had caused me to mature and learn heavy responsibility. These circumstances aided my leadership at Rainelle. Under my supervision, our profits increased considerably, although taking into account the men I had replaced, this was no great feat! I negotiated coal sales regularly with two national firms. I also learned how to operate a Caterpillar bulldozer, plus each piece of equipment used in the mining process.

Even at that age, I knew the value of setting goals and objectives in any business endeavor. So I let my subordinates believe that if we did not maintain our weekly objective of over five thousand tons shipped, we could lose our contracts to a competitor. A bit of a fib, no doubt, but it sure worked since everyone was making good money and no one wanted to see the mine shut down.

One other thing I did was to hire a top-quality mechanic. A highly capable mechanic is probably one of the most important persons on a surface mining or strip job where there is a constant turnover of heavy equipment needing fixed. I'd learned of the top mechanic working for a major construction company in Baltimore, Maryland. His name was Ray Young. Without even discussing it with my grandfather, I offered him $800 a month and the use of the company jeep every other weekend to go see his family in Baltimore.

> A highly capable mechanic is probably one of the most important persons on a surface mining or strip job where there is a constant turnover of heavy equipment needing fixed.

Don't forget, that was more money than I made! But Ray Young's skill was such that the downtime on our fourteen-plus pieces of heavy equipment was reduced by fifty percent. Simple fact, heavy earth-moving equipment not operating accomplishes nothing. When maintained at full efficiency, it's unbelievable what can be accomplished.

That said, I made my share of mistakes and learned some priceless life lessons. Two in particular both involved the same shovel operator, Tom Campbell, a South Carolina native who had far more years' experience than I at this job. Of course, as a cocky twenty-two-year-old superintendent, I thought I knew pretty much everything. One day while he was operating the shovel, I walked up on the right side of his cab, which was his blind side.

At that very moment, he was swinging the bucket around, working all six levers that controlled its movements. He almost took my head off before he saw me. I might have been the superintendent, but he chewed me out good. "Ray, don't ever do that again! You want to talk to me, you come up on my driving side where I can see you. I can handle this machine with such precision I could knock the cap off your head without touching your hair. But not if I can't see where you are!"

And he certainly could. I was impressed with the precision with which he could synchronize all those levers and all the things that massive bucket could do. Eventually when I learned to operate a shovel myself, I got to where I was competent, but never at the level of Tom Campbell. But the lesson I learned that day, which served me for the rest of my life, was to always be observant, keeping a sharp eye out for what was happening around me and why. That would later stand me in good stead when I was in management leadership and needed to pinpoint just what was the heartbeat of a company.

But the other life lesson Tom Campbell taught me was even more valuable. As mentioned earlier, we had quotas for each shift to maintain our overall goal of five thousand tons a week. When I arrived for either day or night shift, I could see immediately whether they'd been using the small shovel or the large shovel and just how well they were doing at making their quota.

One day I arrived to check on the morning shift. I immediately saw that the large shovel, which Tom Campbell should have been operating, had shut down. Angry that my orders had been ignored, I went running up to the shovel to demand, "Tom, why isn't that shovel moving?"

Tom gave me a look that made clear he was speaking to an idiot before he pointed out, "See that boulder over there, Ray? It's made of granite. If I went ahead and tried to move it, we'd have a broken shovel. Which you'd have known if you'd been around this place as long as I have."

I couldn't respond angrily because I knew he was right. But I decided then and there that never again was I going to display my inadequacy as a leader by coming onto a scene and offering my comments before bothering to find out what was going on. All in all, I can't put a price on the experience I gained working for my grandfather at Rainelle Coal Company. If I'd been older, I think I could have managed the business even better. Live and learn!

When Rainelle had exhausted its coal leases, Grandfather Gentry offered to pay for my return to college if I wanted to finish my degree at Virginia Polytechnic Institute. I declined his offer and made a counter-offer. "I've made money for you. Now I want to form my own coal company."

I proposed using a portion of his leased equipment to mine a lease I had secured in Hines, WV. My grandfather agreed. "But we go in as partners, fifty-fifty."

Thus was born the Ray Coal Company. At just twenty-three years old, with some help from my grandfather, I was going into business for myself. I will admit I was an overconfident, brash young man, but it wouldn't take long for life to knock me down a peg.

CHAPTER FIVE

FAILING OR FAILURE?

I waited patiently for the Lord, and He . . . heard my
cry. He also brought me up out of a horrible pit, out
of the miry clay, and set my feet upon a rock, and
established my steps.

—Psalm 40:1-2

If my career was going well, I couldn't say as much for my
marriage. It turned out that as a husband, I'd promised
a lot more than I delivered. Beginning with our first
home. If you look at historical pictures of Rainelle, you'll see
a very small town set in the bottom of a mountain basin. The
mountain slopes, covered with thick deciduous forest, rise
steeply from the flat valley floor.

Our one-room cabin was up on one of those slopes, nestled
picturesquely into the mountains at 3200 feet elevation. It
was originally built for summer rental to families vacationing
from the coastal heat, since Greenbrier County's national
forests, parks, lakes and other nature attractions made the
area a popular summer tourist destination. When Donna and
I moved in, it was full winter, and since it wasn't insulated to
accommodate winter residents, temperatures inside could
drop well below freezing.

Temperatures at the mine site were just as bad. Five days a week in our small kitchen, Donna would fix me a thermos of hot tea and a grilled cheese sandwich for lunch. By noon on the job, the sandwich would be frozen. That's how cold it was.

But at least I had my work. While I spent more than seventy hours a week at the mine, Donna was left stranded in our small, chilly cabin with no one to talk to. To say her days were lonely is an understatement. We were only in the cabin for about two months before moving to a small apartment within the town limits of Rainelle itself. Today, Rainelle's population is around fifteen hundred, and back then it was maybe half that. So there wasn't much for entertainment and even less companionship for Donna while I was gone till late each evening. Even to this day, she complains about our time in Rainelle. It was no way to start a marriage.

It didn't help matters that while we were dating Donna thought she needed to impress me, so she bought a fur coat from her sister for $180, a huge sum for us in those days. Later—too late—she would realize that expensive, ostentatious outfits made no difference to me at all. She regrets the purchase to this day.

A side note about Donna's sister, Margie. By our wedding, Margie had married and moved to Cincinnati. After spending the first night of our honeymoon in Huntington, WV, Donna and I boarded a train the next day to Cincinnati. We became friends with Margie and her husband. Their daughter, Debbie, is like a daughter to us and still calls us every week.

When I did get home from work, I would take Donna out for dinner at a boarding house owned by Meadow River

Lumber Company. For $1.50 each, we would get a feast in the center of the table—about eight vegetables and three meats. I thought I was giving her a big treat, but Donna didn't see it the same way I did. I guess when you're an attractive young lady and twenty lumberjacks are staring at you while you eat, you're going to be uncomfortable.

But we did have some good times and sweet memories in the coal regions. Our daughter, Rebecca Jean Kerwood, was born February 10, 1950. She was absolutely the cutest little girl with golden ringlets, looking much like the child star of that era, Shirley Temple. But even the joy of a daughter was not unalloyed because Becky, as we called her, did not learn to sleep through the night like other babies or even for a few hours. Donna would rock her up to three hours before she'd finally go to sleep. Then fifteen minutes later, she'd wake up again, screaming as loud as possible. Donna's prayer became, "Lord, if I could just sleep through just one night!"

> But we did have some good times and sweet memories in the coal regions. Our daughter, Rebecca Jean Kerwood, was born February 10, 1950.

I should add that her praying did not signify we were now church-goers or living in any way a Christian life. We were both good, moral, honest, hard-working people, and we didn't really see a need for more than that.

Becky around age 3

Eventually, when Becky was about a year old, she grew out of the screaming and began sleeping normally. Some of my sweetest memories of those days are when Donna and I would walk hand-in-hand with Becky in the evening down to the center of Rainelle. We would make it a family excursion, stopping at the drugstore where we'd purchase a twenty-five-cent Wonder book for Becky, while Donna and I split a coke. In her little red coat with her blonde hair curling wildly, Becky could have stepped off the movie screen of a Shirley Temple movie. We adored her, and at those times at least, all was right with the world.

The same could not be said for the coal business. Only three months after the Ray Coal Company went into business, the price of coal dropped from $7.05 a ton to $3.65 a ton, and suppliers were now allowed to sell it only three days a week. Compare that to the years just after WW2 when there was such a shortage of coal that suppliers could name their price. Supply and demand had favored the coal companies, but no longer.

I learned quickly that the coal business was feast or famine. Compounding the problem, strikes by the United Mine Workers would shut down all mines for a couple of months at a time. Harry Truman was president at this time, and he called these strikes a threat to national security. Labor leader John L. Lewis was the star of the coal mines in those days. His authority could shut a mine down with a phone call.

This happened to the Ray Coal Company in 1950, but I just ignored the order. When the local union leader noticed that I had not stopped production, I found a sign at our job site one morning that read: *Here Today, Gone Tomorrow.* Punctuating his point with a personal visit to the mine, the union leader threatened, "If you don't shut the job down, your equipment might suffer some damage tomorrow."

"My equipment is rented," I told him, "and I can't afford to pay for it if I can't sell coal."

"I warned you," he said.

Ray Coal Company was already on the brink of going broke, so rather than risk damage to my rented equipment, I shut down operations and returned the machines. It was only a matter of time before we would have had to shut down anyway.

To complicate life, Donna was not doing well physically. She'd endured several miscarriages. I remember one time when she began bleeding heavily around midnight. I'd rushed her to the nearest hospital seventy miles away. But since I had work commitments, I had to leave her in the maternity ward (there were no individual rooms then unless you were wealthy enough to pay for one). I was not able to return until late afternoon, by which time she'd lost the child. I always regretted not staying with her.

Then about a year-and-a-half after Becky was born, Donna became pregnant again. This time she carried the baby without incident for about seven months. At that time, we had no electric washing machine, so Donna was doing all washing by hand. She was dipping a bucket into the bathtub, which she'd filled with water to do the washing, when the strain of lifting the bucket caused a sharp twinge in her abdomen. Soon after, she went into labor. Once again, I had to drive her seventy miles to the hospital.

Our second daughter was born a few hours later. We named her Ellen Kay. She weighed less than three pounds, a weight at which in those days a newborn seldom survived. Ellen Kay was no exception. Donna blamed herself for the premature birth, but she could have as easily blamed me for not providing her with an easier, safer way to wash clothes. We both grieved the loss of Ellen Kay, but Donna especially had a rough time recovering from the loss.

To illustrate how poor we were at the time, I still have my 1951 tax return, which lists my annual income as *negative* $2500. Donna's family, especially her father, didn't offer much support in this difficult time. One example demonstrates the kind of guy Lester was. He worked at the time for Amhurst Coal Company. He managed to acquire two circular fans from them for just $5 each, as the company had replaced them with new fans. He asked me if I wanted one.

> I still have my 1951 tax return, which lists my annual income as *negative* $2500.

"Sure!" I responded immediately. At that time, our home was scorching hot in the summer since we had no air conditioner. Even one fan could make a big difference.

"Fine," Lester said. "You can have it for five dollars."

So much for thinking it was a gift! Lester knew just how broke we were because we were driving an old coupe with tires that were so bald they barely held the road. Since we could barely afford gas, we would put the vehicle into neutral when we reached the top of a hill, letting it coast down to save fuel.

"I've only got four dollars," I told him.

Lester ended up letting me take the fan for that and owe him the other dollar. I never did get around to paying it, but it made me angry that Lester cared more about a buck than his daughter's needs. And in later years after Lester passed away, Donna and I covered a significant portion of her mother Alma's expenses for her remaining years, so I figure I more than repaid that dollar!

As the Ray Coal Company reached its end, one incident remains a vivid memory even today. It offers a picture of my determination. Or maybe just plain stubbornness. Since I had rented equipment for my business endeavor, I had to return it. But the large equipment shovel had become mired in a sinkhole, so I had to dislodge it first. I pumped water out of the swamp where it was stuck. Then it rained, refilling the swamp with water.

This cycle continued for five days. On the sixth day, I finally freed the shovel. My company might be going under, but I would go down swinging. I was determined to succeed at something, even if just dislodging a piece of equipment from a sinkhole.

It was after this incident that I made a firm resolve. No matter what, I would not put my wife and family through this kind of humiliating predicament ever again. It was grossly unfair to them. Ever since my venture into coal mining had ended, I'd tried to put on a good front. But in truth, I had a hard time coming to terms with the complete debacle of my attempts to provide for my family. I felt like a failure as I worked a variety of short-term jobs, waiting for the next opportunity to come my way. But I have come to believe that you can have a failing experience and not necessarily be a failure.

Better times were on the horizon.

CHAPTER SIX

GETTING BACK UP

.**••**..**••**..**••**..**••**.

Consider it pure joy, my brothers and sisters, whenever you face trials of many kinds, because you know that the testing of your faith produces perseverance. Let perseverance finish its work so that you may be mature and complete (NIV).

—James 1:2-4

If coal mining taught me anything, it was perseverance. It also built character. Like a stubborn boxer who's been knocked down five rounds straight and just keeps staggering back to his feet, I refused to accept defeat. Even after the demise of Ray Coal Company, I continued trying to mine coal with a borrowed 24-inch auger. I partnered with a man I had worked with at Ray Coal. Our plan was to set the auger at the side of the coal seam and bore straight in.

The problem with this method is that if the seam doesn't run level, the auger can trespass above or below, running into shale. If shale mixes with the coal, the coal has to be discarded. True to my luck at coal mining, this turned out to be our experience. An uneven running seam meant we had to cease operation.

For the next four months, I went to work for another company, mining coal from a small drift mine. A drift mine is a type of underground coal mine, as opposed to the surface strip mines I'd worked with for my grandfather and my own company. But instead of sinking shafts down into the ground to dig out the coal, a drift mine dug horizontally, typically into the side of a mountain, to follow the seam of coal.

> Instead of sinking shafts down into the ground to dig out the coal, a drift mine dug horizontally, typically into the side of a mountain, to follow the seam of coal.

This mine was only thirty-eight inches high, since that was the height of the seam. Since I am six-foot-four, I spent a good amount of time squatting inside the mine. I would drill a hole into the coal face about two inches in diameter and three feet deep, then shove a stick of dynamite all the way down into the hole. The charge would explode, breaking up the coal. I would then load the coal into a wheeled cart. Ponies pulled the carts out of the mine to the tipple, a large container where six or eight tons of coal could be stored. From there, trucks hauled the coal to the railroad.

All this work for $3.65 a ton! I'd never realized until then just how much a ton of something was. Nor did I see at the time what this job was building in me. I was more concerned with watching where I stepped after those ponies went by than appreciating all that I was learning. Each evening I returned home coated in black coal dust, so that all Donna could see of me were my eyeballs. The coal dust was everywhere inside the mine, and nobody wore masks. Many miners ended up getting "black lung" disease from long exposure to the coal dust. I believe I didn't suffer that fate only because my stint in the drift mine was a short one.

I then found part-time work operating a bulldozer. As I left for work one morning, I asked Donna to go to the meat market to ask for ten dollars credit in order to buy groceries. A little store like that would carry business on the books, keeping track on a sheet of paper of who owed what. When Donna did as I asked, they asked her what I did for a living. When she told them, they turned her down. They would not give credit to anyone in the coal business. It was a strong message to me.

One other matter made our financial straits even more dire. One of the pieces of equipment I'd acquired while Ray Coal Company was still a growing enterprise was a TD18 bulldozer. Its six thousand dollar price tag was a major investment for a fledgling company like mine. But I really needed its heavy-duty shovel for the type of strip-mining we were doing, so I purchased the TD18 on credit from a man named Dan Houck. We made a handshake deal that I'd pay it off from our coal sales at a hundred dollars a month.

Unfortunately, before I could even pick up the bulldozer, the United Mine Workers strike closed down my company. I called Dan Houck up to see if he'd be willing to undo the deal, since I hadn't even taken possession of the bulldozer. Dan refused.

"Look, it's touch and go with me right now," he told me. "I've already made financial commitments based on my deal with you."

"But I can't use it anymore," I responded. "If I can't mine coal, I have no use for the bulldozer, and I have no way to pay for it."

He wouldn't budge. Instead, he told me flatly, "You know, one thing I've heard about you, Ray Kerwood, is that you're known in this area to be a man of your word. You shook my hand on that deal and gave me your word. Now what are you going to do about it?"

> "One thing I've heard about you, Ray Kerwood, is that you're known in this area to be a man of your word."

I went and picked up the bulldozer. For the next two years, I came up with a hundred dollars each month to pay for a bulldozer I couldn't use. With as little income as we had, it felt like I was paying in my own blood. Only after two years, when I'd paid the purchase price down to forty-five hundred dollars, did Dan Houck finally agree to take the bulldozer back, since he could sell it for more than I still owed on it. That was a time when a handshake meant something, and if it was a difficult period, I could at least hold my head high that my reputation of being a man of my word had not been sullied.

This was the situation I found myself in when my next opportunity came along. Through some friends in

Charleston, I learned that General Motors was taking applications for automobile insurance adjusters. Interviews would be soon. I traveled to Charleston to apply. After undergoing three days of tests, I returned to our small apartment in Rainelle to wait for the results. Two days later, the manager of the General Motors insurance division called to talk to me.

"I have some news," he said.

The manager drove all the way up to Rainelle to interview me personally. He had good news and bad news. The good news—I was one of two people chosen for the job out of ninety-eight applicants.

"What's the bad news?" I asked.

The manager explained that current wage restrictions would not allow them to pay new hires more than $195 a month. So I would be expected to work no more than sixty hours a week and receive no overtime. As an added benefit, I would get a new Chevrolet every two years. Donna and I discussed it briefly and decided we had no choice. I took the job. After all was said and done, I was making only about 78 cents an hour on that job. But at least I got a new car every two years.

For the next month, I was sent to Flint, Michigan, for training at the General Motors plant on the ins and outs of the automotive industry and how to create an accurate adjustor's claim. Then I was assigned to Huntington, WV, as my territory to cover for GM.

Huntington was about a hundred and twenty miles from Rainelle and fifty-plus from Charleston. Donna and I rented an apartment there for fifty-five dollars a month. Added to that expense were utilities, food, clothing, doctors, and any other need, so our finances were once again mighty tight. As an adjuster, I was allotted lunch money of up to two dollars a day. Over the next year, I kept my lunches skimpy, so I could save what was left over. Sometimes you do what you have to do.

I also worked my tail off, trusting that my extra effort would quickly result in receiving a promotion to a more livable wage. Besides myself, there were twelve other claims adjusters, and within a short time, I found myself typically handling more claims than any of the others, averaging from thirty-five to forty claims a month.

We ended up moving twice more while we lived in Huntington, the first time because the apartment we'd rented turned out to have a mice infestation. Shortly after we moved to our second apartment, Donna's father paid us a visit. We were in the process while he was there of turning on the natural gas for our furnace. As I went through the process, Lester explained to me that as you turn the valve crossways in the three-quarter-inch pipe, the gas would shut off. After his first explanation, he stopped, then said, "Now let me review this very carefully."

And he did. To be ornery, I then asked him to go over it one more time. Lester was already of the opinion that I was the dumbest son-in-law his daughter could have brought into the family, so he went through the process at length an extra time. Later on, I learned that he'd told his wife, "Donna's fellow Ray, he's going to get the whole family blown up."

> Later on, I learned that he'd told his wife, "Donna's fellow Ray, he's going to get the whole family blown up."

Lester certainly didn't think much of me, especially once my coal business failed. But the only evidence I could think of to offset his negative opinion was my earlier success of steering that tanker into port. Regardless of that particular achievement, I couldn't deny the truth that I was a college dropout. I'd always rather regretted not taking my grandfather up on his offer to pay for me to go back to college. But by then, Donna was pregnant, so sticking to coal mining had seemed the better choice.

In any case, I figured I'd probably have flunked out. In high school, I was just a football hero. I'd graduated with a good GPA, but higher math always got the best of me, as that navigation course at the Merchant Marine Academy demonstrated. I did take analytical geometry during the year I attended college, but only because it was taught by a nice-looking instructor. And I flunked the course twice! With subjects like psychology and economics, I did really well, but higher math I just couldn't finesse.

In the end, I did pretty well even without that college degree. And I was far more concerned about Donna's opinion of me than her father's. I was even more determined to ensure that my wife and family never again suffered want because of my inability to provide, and even if it meant skimping on my own lunches, we were doing okay. Enough that in 1952, Donna and I bought our first luxury. This was a twenty-inch black-and-white television console, purchased with a loan for three hundred dollars from GMAC (General Motors Acceptance Corporation, now Ally Financial, originally founded by GM to offer financing so customers could buy their cars and other products). We managed to pay off that loan in just one year at twenty-five dollars a month. Our entertainment was now taken care of very inexpensively—professional football for me and all the rest of the programming for Donna.

CHAPTER SEVEN

A GOOD INHERITANCE

O Lord, You are the portion of my inheritance and my cup. You maintain my lot. The lines have fallen to me in pleasant places. Yes, I have a good inheritance.

—Psalm 16:5-6

A good percentage of my adjustment claims for General Motors took place at one dealership, Rich Chevrolet in Huntington. I got to know most of their management through these regular visits, so when their service manager moved on, they offered me his job. The salary was almost twice the money I'd been making, so I accepted the position, starting in early 1953.

I worked at Rich Chevrolet for more than two years. As the service manager, I was responsible for the entire service and parts departments, which included eight mechanics, four men who did body work, and one painter. Keeping the owner, my subordinates, and the customers all happy made this a challenging job. Now I was on the other side of the adjusting process, making estimates for Rich Chevrolet. The prior manager had made the estimates high, with the owner's blessing, because this resulted in bigger commissions.

That was not my method. I lowered the bids to fair estimates. Instead of hurting the company, this paid off because we ended up with twice the business when customers saw that we were honest. Everyone benefited in the end. The company profited, my own commission increased, and the customer was treated fairly. This level of integrity would see me through future business dealings with favorable results.

I was working at Rich Chevrolet when Donna gave birth to our second child and first son, Stephen Kenna Kerwood, on March 10th, 1954. If finances remained tight, this was a time of peace and stability in our family life. "Pleasant places" and "a good inheritance" is how King David describes it in Psalm 16:6. Donna and I loved our children dearly and loved each other. Donna was an excellent mother. Becky started school not long after Stephen was born and proved an excellent student, as our sons in turn would demonstrate in later years.

The only negative that comes to mind during this time period was that Donna suffered a severe allergic reaction to the chemicals involved in washing diapers and other clothing as well as standard housecleaning products. She was always a conscientious wife and mother, keeping our house immaculate and working hard to take care of our children. All of which involved a lot of having her hands in water and various cleaning solutions. No matter what creams or lotions she tried, her hands were always chapped and raw, often even bleeding, which in turn was quite painful. Nothing the doctors prescribed helped either. But we were grateful for two healthy children, a roof over our heads, and an income that put food on the table, if not a lot of extras.

I was not spiritually sensitive enough at that time to direct my gratitude to God. Still, though I didn't recognize it then, God was already at work in my life, guiding me on a path I couldn't have taken on my own. I'm just an average person. But during my life there have been times of great favor, and not because of any special business acumen on my part, happenstance, or pure luck. Times that I can only describe as divine intervention. More than what I deserve.

> Though I didn't recognize it then, God was already at work in my life, guiding me on a path I couldn't have taken on my own.

One of these happenings occurred in September, 1955, while I was still working at Rich Chevrolet. I learned through an ad in the *Charleston Gazette* that Gulf Oil Corporation was seeking a sales engineer to cover territory in West Virginia and Virginia. The ad stated that no applicant would be considered without an engineering degree and that interviews would cease at 5 p.m. on the very same day I was reading the advertisement.

I considered my circumstances. It was a fifty-mile drive to the site of the interview, and since I didn't have a college degree, it was unlikely I'd be considered as a candidate for the job anyway. I decided to go for it. At 4 p.m., I still had ten to fifteen cars to deal with before closing, along with all the paperwork. My associate manager at the time, Jim Lute, was willing to finish the day's business for me, but I began making excuses.

"I could hardly make it in time," I told him. "I wouldn't get the job anyway. Besides, it's not fair to you. So I've decided not to go."

He insisted I go, certain that I could do better for my family than my current position.

"Don't worry. I'll handle everything here," he assured me.

I've never forgotten his encouragement. Without it, I would never have gone for the interview. I arrived at the Daniel Boone Hotel in Charleston at five minutes after 5 o'clock. As I sat there waiting, I overheard the interviewer say to the applicant before me, "If you'd shut your mouth, I'll answer the question."

I already didn't feel good about my prospects. That exchange only added to my anxiety. What chance did I have? I was five minutes late, had no degree, and the interviewer didn't sound very nice. What had I gotten myself into?

When that interview finished, the interviewer came out and barked at me, "What are you doing here?"

For whatever reason, he agreed reluctantly to interview me. I told him about my experience in charge of heavy equipment for Rainelle, my work in the coal mines, plus the month I'd spent learning about cars at General Motors Tech in Flint, Michigan, and my current position as service manager at a Chevrolet dealership. I was pretty good at talking myself up, and I must have come off pretty effectively, convincing Gulf that they would be "honored" to have such an outstanding applicant. I laugh now when I think about my bravado.

Gulf Oil eventually paid my airfare to Philadelphia, where I was hired by the regional manager. It was the start of twenty-eight years working for Gulf Oil in various roles. This would turn out to be a pivotal time in my life. I'd left a job with little-to-no future prospects to join a national company worth billions of dollars with more than fifty thousand employees. Where my future led now would be dependent on my performance, and since I was used to hard work, I wasn't worried about that part. Surely, this was not happenstance, but providence.

After three months of training, I was assigned to the southern West Virginia area, covering fleets, coal mines, and interstate road contractors. For the next eight years, my territory expanded into parts of Virginia and Kentucky. I won several sales awards with commensurate recognition.

Another thing I did during this time period was to take a night course at Marshall University. Held on Thursday evenings, the course was on psychology in the business industry and covered topics like morale and leadership qualities. You were supposed to have a psychology degree to take the course. Since I didn't have one, I audited it. I made every class and studied until my eyes crossed, even though I wasn't getting credit. In fact, one time when traveling for work, I drove a hundred and fifty-two miles through a snowstorm so as not to miss a class.

I ended up with an A-minus. To me, this was a big deal because it made me realize I had potential I had never utilized. Maybe not in math, but I could hold my own in other areas. This gave me a leg up. Confidence. I took what I learned and put it into practice on the job. One time I gave a speech to four hundred people, based on content from that class. Afterwards, I was strongly complimented by the regional manager, and the speech ended up being a significant factor to my later receiving a promotion.

> I was strongly complimented by the regional manager, and the speech ended up being a significant factor to my later receiving a promotion.

Like I said before, I would always regret not finishing college. A college degree is a big asset in any industry. But I also learned to compensate for it. For one, I refused to act like a college dropout. Just like that Gulf Oil interview. I should never have been allowed in there without an engineering degree. But I knew what my IQ was and that I had the goods, so I went for it. Whoever I've worked for, I'd watch what they did and say to myself, "Man, they put their pants on same as I do! If they can do it, I can do it." That competitiveness definitely gave me an edge that helped make up for a lack of college degree.

Since I was now on the road overseeing a vast area, there was no longer any real need for me to be stationed in Huntington. So in 1957, Donna and I moved to Charleston, where we could be closer to family and old friends. There we bought our first house at 128 Costello Street. The entire cost was $9500, and thanks to our careful saving over the last few years plus a small loan from family, we were able to put down $1500, a sizeable down-payment in those days. Our mortgage was $80 a month, which was quite a bit more than we'd been paying for our apartment. But my income was now a whopping $4500 a year, which seemed a fortune compared to what we'd been earning when I first started working for General Motors.

I could now say honestly that better times had arrived. Donna and I were both still very cautious with our finances, mindful from past experience of how easily the tables could turn. Donna made every dollar stretch, and we were conscientious to put money into savings. But we no longer had to worry each month about paying our basic bills, and that in itself was a great stress relief.

Still, if my career had taken an upward turn, my spiritual life was definitely a work-in-progress. Being hired by Gulf Oil would prove the pivotal event that changed forever my professional future. I would soon meet a man whose impact on my spiritual future—and Donna's—would prove just as pivotal.

CHAPTER EIGHT

INFLUENCED FOR ETERNITY

Good Teacher, what shall I do that I may inherit
eternal life?

—Mark 10:17

L et me back up just a bit here to expound a little more
in depth on my church background. I've mentioned
attending an Episcopalian church off and on as a boy.
My mother didn't attend church herself. As a working single
mom with three children, she enjoyed Sunday as her day off.
But she did feel it was important for us kids to develop a
religious and moral framework, so she would send us on our
own.

By my teens I wasn't attending church anymore, though
I'd acquired a Book of Common Prayer, which I did carry with
me even while at sea during the war and would read from
time to time. I had enough consciousness of God to thank
Him for sparing my life when I almost lost my arm and when
I narrowly escaped being swept overboard.

What I did take away from my upbringing was a strong
sense of right and wrong. While other sailors in the Merchant
Marines were going off with women, getting drunk, or

indulging in other questionable behavior, I refrained because I knew it wasn't right and I also believed that God would disapprove of such behavior. So I guess that means I certainly believed in God, just as when I begged forgiveness for cussing in that cornfield. But that was where my spiritual life ended. I knew God existed. I tried to live the kind of decent, moral life that God expected. But I was missing something.

In essence, I knew *about* God, but I didn't *know* God personally. Scripture describes this situation quite vividly and makes abundantly clear that just believing in God's existence isn't good enough if you haven't chosen to know Him and follow Him:

> You believe that there is one God. You do well. Even the demons believe—and tremble!
>
> —James 2:19

If my own childhood church attendance had been sporadic, Donna had actually grown up attending church. Her mother was a godly Christian woman, and during Donna's growing-up years, she'd attended several different churches with her daughters. In her teen years, Donna even attended a revival service with a friend, during which both responded to the altar call, going forward to pray the sinner's prayer and accept Jesus.

Donna would later admit she'd gone forward only because it was expected and she'd felt pressured. Her father was certainly not a God-fearing man, and by the time we were married, Donna was as disinterested in church attendance and religion as I was. Still, she had more knowledge of theology and the Bible than I did.

By now, we'd been married almost exactly ten years, and I'd been with Gulf Oil for a couple of years. We had two beautiful children, Becky now seven years old and Stephen three. Our financial situation was secure. But Donna and I were having some difficulties in our marriage. I don't even remember now what they were in particular. Perhaps the stress of my long absences on the road. The constant pain and itching Donna was suffering from her skin condition didn't help. Either way, God used those difficulties in our marriage to finally start getting my attention.

> God used those difficulties in our marriage
> to finally start getting my attention.

The first happening God used to grab my attention was an invitation to an event Donna and I attended at the Charleston Airport, where a Pastor Melvin Efaw was scheduled to preach. The invitation came through a man named Wallace, who played the piano and led the choir at a Presbyterian church just down the hill from our house. He was canvassing door to door and happened to catch Donna and me at home. He handed us an invitation, told us there'd be a free dinner, and asked if we'd like to come.

Since neither Donna nor I attended church, why we said yes is still a bit of a mystery. But we did go. Pastor Melvin spoke on various attributes of Jesus Christ, showing how

Jesus Himself claimed in the Gospels to be the Water of Life, the Bread of Life, the Good Shepherd, the Resurrection and the Life. I had never heard such preaching, and Pastor Melvin's description of the person of Jesus Christ roused such a yearning in my soul that I left in tears, though I didn't respond to the altar call to accept Jesus as my Savior.

Still, Pastor Melvin's preaching had roused in me a desire to attend church again. On Sunday mornings, I began walking the few short blocks from our home down the hill to the Presbyterian church. With small kids to care for, Donna wasn't interested, so I went alone. Perhaps a month into my attendance there, I decided to visit the adult Sunday school class as well. A man named C.W. Lee was teaching the class. He wasn't a clergyman, but a lab technician with Union Carbide. I found out later that he didn't even attend that church. But he was so knowledgeable about Scripture and such a powerful Bible teacher that the Presbyterian church had invited him to teach their adult Sunday school class.

I was very impressed with C. W. Lee's teaching. The following Sunday, I went back to his class. Before the class started, I hovered close by, hoping for an opportunity to talk with him. When the opportunity came, I shared briefly with him that my wife and I were experiencing some difficulties in our marriage. Would he be willing someday to visit with Donna and me?

I hadn't really thought this through, so I was taken aback when C. W. responded immediately, "Sure! How about tonight?"

Donna was far from happy when I came home from church and let her know we'd be hosting guests that evening. "Why on earth would you do that?" she demanded.

"I don't know!" I admitted. "Something just prompted me to do it."

"So what do we do?" she asked in a panic. "What will we say?"

By that time, I too was in a bit of a panic and wishing I'd never invited C. W. over. "We'll just ask him questions," I reassured Donna, "and hopefully he'll move on pretty quickly."

That evening, Donna and I were waiting nervously when C.W. arrived. He'd brought with him his wife Ruth. By the time we'd all exchanged greetings, it was clear to Donna and me both that this couple was different from anyone we'd ever known. More pertinently, it was also clear that Jesus was the center of their life. Within a short time, C. W. had his Bible open and was explaining to us just what it meant to know God personally and to receive Jesus Christ as Savior and Lord. First he read John 3:16 to us:

> For God so loved the world that He gave His only begotten Son, that whoever believes in Him should not perish but have everlasting life.
>
> —John 3:16

I'd heard those words before, but somehow on this evening it sank into my heart as never before that God, my Creator, the Ruler of this Universe, actually loved, not just all of humanity generically, but *me* personally, enough to send His Son Jesus Christ to be born on this earth. I could see on Donna's face that she was responding to this message as intensely as I was.

C.W. then took us through a series of verses from the New Testament epistle of Romans. We would later learn these verses are popularly termed the *Roman Road* and are an easy, effective way to share the Gospel as each verse leads to the next to create a direct road pointing straight to Jesus Christ. The first verse was Romans 3:23:

> For all have sinned and fall short of the glory of God.
>
> —Romans 3:23

That wasn't hard for me to agree with. I might have lived a fairly moral life, but I was only too aware of how far I'd fallen short of God's expectations, in my marriage above all. But if that was a depressing realization, C. W. didn't leave us long without hope. He turned the page to Romans 5:8:

> But God demonstrates His own love toward us, in that while we were still sinners, Christ died for us.
>
> — Romans 5:8

C.W. explained that the reason God had sent His Son to the cross was to pay the penalty that I and every other human being deserved for our sins. He then showed us just what that penalty was from Romans 6:23:

> For the wages of sin is death, but the gift of God is eternal life in Christ Jesus our Lord.
>
> —Romans 6:23

I knew only too well that I too deserved that penalty, no matter how good and moral a life I tried to live. But if I deserved the wages of death, how exactly did I go about exchanging those wages for the gift of eternal life? C. W. answered my question by turning to Romans 8:1:

> There is therefore now no condemnation to those who are in Christ Jesus.
>
> —Romans 8:1

C. W. explained to Donna and me how Jesus, the sinless Son of God, had freely offered His life in our stead on the cross, so that through His sacrifice, we might be saved from condemnation and declared righteous and cleansed from sin before a holy God. C. W. then went on to read Romans 10:9-10:

> That if you confess with your mouth the Lord Jesus and believe in your heart that God has raised Him from the dead, you will be saved. For with the heart one believes unto righteousness, and with the mouth confession is made unto salvation.
>
> —Romans 10:9-10

I didn't need C. W. to explain that it was now my turn. That I needed to make the decision to not just believe *about* God, but to believe *in* Him with all my heart and to confess publicly my faith in God's Son Jesus Christ as my Lord and Savior. Beside me, I could see Donna had made the same decision. Kneeling together, Donna and I both prayed aloud, asking forgiveness for our sins and asking Jesus into our hearts, acknowledging Him from that moment forward as our Lord and Savior.

When we rose from our knees, Donna and I both knew without the smallest doubt that we were now gloriously saved. C. W. then read to us the last verses that were part of the *Roman Road*:

> I beseech you therefore, brethren, by the mercies of God, that you present your bodies a living sacrifice, holy, acceptable to God, which is your reasonable service. And do not be conformed to this world, but be transformed by the renewing of your mind, that you may prove what is that good and acceptable and perfect will of God
>
> —Romans 12:1-2

C. W. and Ruth then spent some time explaining to Donna and me just what it meant to live our lives as daily sacrifices to God and to let the Holy Spirit transform our minds so that we would no longer be conformed to the sinful world around us, but would be able to follow God's perfect will for our lives.

After C. W. and Ruth left that night, Donna and I headed upstairs to bed. We were so happy, all the little differences that had been dividing us just dissolved into vapor. Just three steps up the staircase was a small landing. Donna, who was climbing the stairs ahead of me, suddenly stopped and turned to look down at me. With amazement in her voice, she asked, "Ray, do you realize the significance of what just happened?"

Maybe we didn't know then the complete significance of what had just happened to us, but we both knew this was the most important event that had ever happened in either of our lives. C. W. later told us that of all the people with whom he'd shared the Gospel, he'd never met two so ready to meet Jesus. We were like two ripe cherries just waiting to be picked, he added with a smile.

Certainly, this was not how either Donna or I could have dreamed our evening would end. That brief encounter with a S. S. teacher who didn't even attend the same church. C. W.'s immediate offer to visit our home. That Donna and I both, who'd never so much as discussed spiritual things together, would be willing to listen to an evangelism presentation from a total stranger, much less be immediately drawn to its truth. It was all so completely outside the norm for our lives to this point that I can only describe it as a miracle.

Donna and I can both look back now and pinpoint that evening as the pivotal moment of our lives. It has influenced us for eternity. It changed every aspect of our lives. From then on, we lived differently, thought differently, planned differently, acted differently.

Chapter Nine

Healing and Growing

"For I will restore health to you and heal you of your wounds," says the Lord.

—Jeremiah 30:17

Perhaps the biggest tangible impact on our lives was what to this day Donna and I consider another miracle, and that is the healing of Donna's hands. We'd tried every possible treatment to deal with the allergic reactions that were at times so bad they left her skin looking like raw meat. One time I drove her all the way to Louisville, Kentucky, to see a dermatologist we had heard about. He put a bunch of needles in Donna's back to see what she was allergic to, but with no result.

Not long after that evening with C. W. and Ruth Lee, I was having lunch with a manager from the General Motors insurance division, who told me he knew a dermatology specialist in Charleston. We scraped up enough money to go see this man. He told us the previous approach had been all wrong. He performed a procedure that abraded away all the dead skin, leaving new, healthy skin to grow. He also told us that stress was a contributing factor.

Sure enough, between the doctor's new treatments and Donna finding peace through God, her hands cleared up in six months. To us, this was a clear message of how our heavenly Father intervenes in tangible ways in the daily lives of His children.

After leading Donna and me to Christ, C. W. and Ruth Lee didn't just walk away, but poured themselves into helping us grow as Christians. This is even more significant because we were complete strangers to them before that night, and both of them were so busy, C. W. especially, I don't know how they found time to do all they did, much less add on becoming our own spiritual mentors.

C.W. not only worked full-time at Union Carbide and taught Sunday school, but he also found time to serve on the board of Youth for Christ, the local committee for Child Evangelism Fellowship, as superintendent for Union Mission, a ministry to the homeless and needy in downtown Charleston, as well as with the local chapter of Christian Business Men's Committee. C. W. was a very mild-mannered man, but not shy at all, constantly sharing his faith at every opportunity. His place of employment, Union Carbide, had six thousand employees, and it was a bit of a joke that he'd witnessed to every one of them.

Certainly, it seemed everyone knew C. W. Anytime we went out for lunch together, he would speculate about the people around us—who was saved and who needed the Lord. But he wouldn't just speculate. He'd find a way to strike up a conversation. Eventually, he'd ask where they went to church, and pretty soon he'd be sharing the Gospel. To a new Christian like me, it was an eye-opener as I'd never met anyone like him.

> He'd find a way to strike up a conversation. Eventually, he'd ask where they went to church, and pretty soon he'd be sharing the Gospel.

C. W. and Ruth made sure from the beginning that Donna and I got plugged into a good, Bible-teaching church. But their main mentoring program, if that's the right term, consisted basically of taking us with them anywhere they went. If missionaries were in town speaking, they'd take us along to listen. If they heard of any special evangelist speaking somewhere, they would invite Donna and me to join them. Spiritually, we were growing by leaps and bounds.

The biggest impact of this in my own life was C. W. getting me involved in the Christian Business Men's Committee (now known as Christian Business Men's Connection). CBMC was originally started by famed Christian businessman, inventor, and philanthropist R. G. LeTourneau, who also founded LeTourneau University. One day C. W. found out that LeTourneau was coming into Charleston to speak in the auditorium of a large Presbyterian church. The cost for the event was two dollars a person.

"You've been wanting to get active in CBMC," C. W. commented to me. "Why don't you take charge of the ticket sales?"

So I did. I was perhaps a little naïve, as I just kept the money and tickets in a dresser drawer. CBMC members would ask me for ten tickets or twenty. I'd give them the tickets. They'd come back, telling me how many tickets they'd sold and handing me the money, which I stuffed in the drawer, just trusting them that it was the right amount.

When the event happened and I had to give account for the funds, I pulled out the money and remaining tickets. When I counted it all out, I was two dollars short. I figured that was likely my mistake, pulled out two dollars from the six dollars that was all I had in my wallet at the time. That left me just four dollars to get through the week. But it was a great experience, and at that time at least, I had no worries my fellow Christians would ever cheat me or let me down.

Thanks to C.W., I also began meeting other God-fearing Christian men who had a major impact on my life and Christian growth. One of these was Maynard Davis, an investor sales agent who loved to talk about Jesus. He had started the original Charleston CBMC chapter in the same hotel where I was interviewed for my employment with Gulf Oil. Long before I met him, Maynard would show up at the hotel every Thursday morning at 6:30 a.m. and pray for other Christian businessmen to join him. It took several months before he finally had his first member. By the time I joined, there were twenty-five members.

In 1978, Maynard Davis stood up in church to share that the verse he'd chosen for the year was Philippians 3:10: *"that I may know Him [Christ] and His sufferings."* At that time, he already knew he was suffering from terminal cancer. That fall, I received news of his deteriorating health and felt a strong compulsion to visit him immediately. His wife answered the door. She shared with me that Maynard was in hospice care and had come home because he didn't want to die in the hospital. She then led me to his bedroom, where I found Maynard in extreme pain, yet praising the Lord with the words, "Precious Jesus". I visited briefly, then left. It was just a few days later that he passed into glory. His faithfulness in serving God still brings me to tears.

I also met Harry Musser while a member of CBMC. About a year after I started attending, there was a regional meeting in Cleveland. Harry asked if I was going. I knew I didn't have the finances for such a trip, so I told him no. Harry continued to encourage me to attend, mentioning that so-and-so always went and it was always a blessing. He added that he would drive and we could share a room. Beyond that, all I would need was thirty dollars for the meals.

"Harry," I told him, "I only have sixty-five dollars in the bank, and I would feel guilty spending thirty of that on myself."

A short time later, Harry approached me again. "Ray, I know someone who'd like to donate thirty dollars as a scholarship for someone to attend that conference. If I can arrange it, would you take the scholarship?"

"Yes, I'd love to," I told him, surprised.

Harry made the arrangements, and I went with him. It was a wonderful experience. Today almost sixty years later, I can still hear that crowd of a thousand men singing, "How Great Thou Art". Not to mention all those testimonies of lives changed by Jesus Christ. I'd always suspected Harry's father was my benefactor. But many years later, Maynard Davis said to me, "You know that was Harry's money, right?"

I'd always suspected Harry's father was my benefactor. But many years later, Maynard Davis said to me, "You know that was Harry's money, right?"

For thirty dollars, Harry gave me pleasant memories that are still with me to this day. I wanted then to pay those thirty dollars back, but Maynard assured me that would make Harry uncomfortable.

"Why don't you just pay it forward?" he suggested. And that is what I eventually did.

Donna and I both were also impacted profoundly by our relationship with another couple, Walter and Cynthia Pauley. Walter was a deacon in the church we attended, sang in the choir, worked for a prominent home furnishings company as an interior decorator, and was a very accomplished artist. Few people have it all, but Walter was gifted. More significantly, he and Cynthia were committed to serving God.

One evening Cynthia called to ask if Donna would go with her to visit an older woman from the congregation, who was nearly blind. Donna willingly agreed. When they arrived at the woman's house, Donna and Cynthia found the woman in her bathroom. She'd fallen and was wedged between the wall and the commode. An obvious odor emanated from her. Donna and Cynthia cleaned her up and got her back in bed.

Later on as Donna and Cynthia stood out on the woman's porch, Donna told Cynthia with tears in her eyes, "I can't believe you are doing all this! You'll have stars in your crown for sure!"

"No, I won't!" Cynthia replied quickly. "Because this isn't my ministry. It's Walter's."

Cynthia explained that Walter had to work that night, which was why she'd called Donna in the first place. The church had pretty much forgotten the woman, but Walter had continued helping her. Another time, I asked Walter to help my mother furnish her apartment, since this was his profession. She was short on money, and I found out later he'd done her entire apartment at less than cost, adding money from his own pocket to finish the job. As I grew as a Christian, I would continue to meet men of faith like C.W., Maynard, Harry, and Walter, whose spiritual life would challenge and inspire my own.

One other man who really impacted my life during this period wasn't a new acquaintance, but an old one. Leon McCoy had attended high school in Charleston with me, though he'd been a couple grades behind. We'd played football together, but weren't really buddies since Leon was known as the worst renegade in high school. He'd never gone to war, as WW2 had finished by the time he was old enough. But sometime while I was out in the Atlantic on a tanker ship, he'd met a girl whose husband had been killed in the war. She was a Christian and shared her faith with him. Leon became a Christian, and his life totally changed. I still remember one of Leon's favorite sayings: "If I could be Satan's right-hand man, why should I do any less for Jesus?"

Much like the apostle Paul after his Damascus Road encounter (Acts 9), Leon was now sharing his faith with as much gusto as he'd spent getting into trouble. And people listened, saying, "If God can save Leon McCoy, He can save anyone!"

After high school, Leon played football, making All-American. He eventually married the girl who'd led him to Christ and became a high school coach. For years, he held a Bible study for students until protesters against any Christian influence in schools managed to agitate enough to shut him down. When that happened, the local post office overflowed with mail from past students writing in about how he'd changed their lives. I had the privilege of meeting him again at a CBMC retreat where we were both scheduled to give our testimonies. What a special reunion that was!

Of course, when Donna and I became Christians, our family life changed in many ways as well, though in other ways not so much. The biggest change was that church was now a major focal point of our family life. The kids went to Sunday school with us and loved it as much as we did. Becky, who was older, got especially involved in church activities. She showed a love for God from an early age. I've mentioned Donna's sister Margie, who married and moved to Cincinnati. Her daughter Debby still remembers how Becky witnessed to her when Becky was just ten years old.

"I ridiculed her," Debby would share in later years. "But she didn't give up witnessing. In the end, that was the seed that led me to Christ."

Debby recently returned from a missions trip to Trinidad. She's been on other missions trips as well, fruit of Becky's persistent witnessing. Like her mother, grandmothers, and great-grandmothers, Becky was a strong woman, smart, determined, resourceful, and compassionate. She was always a tomboy, playing a lot of sports just like her dad, but otherwise you could see the influence in her life of all those stalwart, doer-type women God has been so gracious as to put in my life from Grandmother Gentry, my mother, wife, all the way down to my precious daughter.

One thing that didn't change was being involved in our kids' lives because Donna and I had already made that a priority. Our son Stephen was quite small for his age until about eleven years old or so, but he played both shortstop and pitcher on a Little League baseball team in Huntington. Though he was small, he was surehanded and would managed to catch the ball just as the runner was sliding into plate and tag him out. When he pitched, he had a curve ball that was notoriously hard to hit.

> One thing that didn't change was being involved in our kids' lives because Donna and I had already made that a priority.

By then I was traveling fifty thousand miles a year as sales engineer for Gulf Oil. But I practiced catch with Steve any time I could and tried to make it to as many of his games as possible. When his team reached the finals and went on to play for the championship games, I remember driving a hundred miles from where I was stationed that particular night so I wouldn't miss his game. I'd made it my goal to be a very different father figure to my children than my father was to me, and despite long hours traveling, I scheduled in as much time as possible to be with my kids as well as with Donna.

We lived in Huntington until 1970. Those were years of spiritual growth, of precious family memories, of an enjoyable, if challenging, job career with Gulf Petroleum. Two major events stand out in our remaining years there.

The first was the birth of our third child and second son, Brian Scott Kerwood, on February 2nd, 1966. This was, frankly, a shock since Donna had just turned forty years old. With Becky well into high school and Stephen now twelve years old, another baby in the home was not even in our thinking, especially after the numerous miscarriages Donna had suffered over the years. It took a while to accept this new upheaval in our plans. Donna had always had difficult pregnancies, and this proved no exception. But by the time Brian was born, we'd grown excited at adding a third child to the family, and of course once we met Brian in person, we all fell in love with him, not just Donna and me, but Becky and Stephen. Becky especially doted on her younger brother and was thrilled to have a baby to play with.

The second significant event, and less happy, though still a blessing, was the death of my mother from cancer in 1967. She had remarried just three years prior, and I'd hoped she'd be with us to see her grandchildren grow up. The blessing came in sharing my faith with her. She'd never been a church-goer, even when she encouraged us to attend as children. But when I spoke with her about salvation and her eternal destiny, her faith in Jesus Christ was evident. She had a Bible with her, and I could see that she'd marked in it John 3:16 and the various verses in Romans through which C. J. had led Donna and me to Christ. When she died, I had peace that she was with her Savior and that one day I will see her again.

Kerwood Family circa 1967

C. J. and Ruth remained our closest of friends as well as spiritual mentors until we moved from West Virginia. Even then, we would talk at least once a year on the phone. C. J. finally passed into God's presence in 2008 at the age of ninety-two. Ruth had passed away a few years prior. By then, he'd impacted thousands of people through his godly life and faithful testimony.

C. J. always told people that when he died, he did not want to leave anything behind. That he wanted to give everything he had to the Lord's work. That's how I remember him.

That's how I want people to remember me.

CHAPTER TEN

THE WORST OF THE WORST

The Lord is my Shepherd . . . He leads me beside the still waters . . . Yea, though I walk through the valley of the shadow of death, I will fear no evil; For You are with me; Your rod and Your staff, they comfort me."

—Psalm 23:1-4

We could not have guessed during those "still waters" of the 1960s how soon we would be walking through the valley of the shadow of death. In 1963, I was promoted to manager in charge of the industrial and commercial market for the West Virginia district of Gulf Oil's operations. In 1968, during a corporate reorganization, I was promoted again, this time to sales manager.

Selling the Charleston house where we'd experienced so many good years, we moved to Baltimore, Maryland, where the new job was based. We also found another good church to attend. My long hours on the road were now ended, as I was now working out of an office, so I had more time to spend with my family, an added bonus to this promotion.

My task for Gulf Oil was to merge three districts—Wilmington, DE, Baltimore, MD, and Washington, D.C.—into one. Not only did I complete the merger, but within two years, our nine sales engineers had increased sales by a hundred percent. Our district led every sales district in Gulf Oil's eastern region.

Becky's First Prom

Becky and Stephen were in high school by now, and though adjusting to a new school had its challenges, they both remained top students with an excellent reputation among their teachers and youth group leaders alike. Becky was teaching Sunday school at church. She graduated from high school and started college at the University of Maryland, earning her own way through scholarships and part-time jobs.

In early January, 1970, I received a call from the central office of Gulf Oil's eastern region in Philadelphia. They wanted me to travel there to be interviewed for a job opportunity, which included being director of the home-heat market of Gulf Oil, U.S.A. as well as vice president of five Gulf Oil home-heat subsidiaries. These various divisions together represented more than a billion dollars of income to Gulf Oil, and the position included responsibility for over four hundred employees.

Before my own interview, I learned that Gulf Oil had interviewed two dozen other managers. I was also told that at this level of management, they never promoted from one market to another market. That ruled me out, since I was working in the industrial/commercial market and this was home heat. Still, the experience of interviewing for the position would be good for me, so I decided to go for it. That I had minimal expectation of being chosen was actually a benefit as I went into the interview completely relaxed with a devil-don't-care attitude.

At the end of the interview, I was told they'd be in touch if they were interested. I headed back to Baltimore and promptly dismissed the whole matter from my mind. So it was a real surprise when a few days later, I received a phone call from the central office. Effective in two weeks, I would be promoted. I was to put my house up for sale and move to Philadelphia as soon as was practical, with all expenses paid.

> It was a real surprise when a few days later, I received a phone call from the central office. Effective in two weeks, I would be promoted.

That should have been a high point of my life, but it was followed almost immediately by tragedy. By this time, our daughter Becky was just starting the second semester of her junior year at the University of Maryland. But our two sons, Steve and Brian, traveled up to Philadelphia with Donna and me as we prepared for the job transition. This included, of course, looking for a new house. Meanwhile, we were staying in a hotel.

We were at the hotel when we received the phone call every parent dreads. Our beautiful twenty-year-old daughter Becky was in the emergency room of a Washington, D.C., hospital, and we needed to get there as soon as possible. The distance from Philadelphia to D.C. was usually about a three-hour drive. Since this was still January, and snow made the roads slick, it took us even longer to reach the hospital. Our vehicle felt weighed down with far more than four people and a trunk full of our belongings. Not knowing our daughter's condition was the hardest part of that drive.

I've said before how Becky resembled Shirley Temple as a toddler with the cutest golden ringlets crowning her head. In those days back in Rainelle, our biggest concern with her was her insomnia, leaving Donna exhausted trying to rock her to sleep. Becky had eventually grown out of that problem and into a self-reliant, confident, and well-adapted young woman. She'd given her life to Jesus Christ at an early age and had always participated wholeheartedly in church and youth group activities. I've already mentioned how even as a young child, Becky was constantly sharing her faith with others.

Becky's ultimate goal was to become a teacher, and by her junior year at UM, she'd already begun her practice teaching. She was also working as a dorm supervisor. Like both of her brothers later on, Becky had never expected a handout from us to put her through college, but worked hard to get scholarships and part-time jobs to pay her tuition. She also studied hard. Just the week before, she'd called Donna. During their conversation, she'd mentioned that she was experiencing very painful headaches.

"You're studying too hard," Donna reassured her. "Try to take it a little easier."

Later that week, Becky called again. She wasn't a complainer, and like I said, she'd been conscientiously working her way through college. But she mentioned to Donna that she hadn't eaten dinner because she didn't have money to go to the cafeteria.

Donna scolded Becky a bit for letting her finances get to such a point without telling us. But as soon as she was off the phone, Donna was writing Becky a letter, into which she slipped twenty dollars to cover Becky's meals till we got back to Baltimore. Becky still had that letter when we reached her, and to this day, I carry it in my wallet, now quite faded and frayed at the edges. The sight of it still brings tears to my eyes.

At the time, though, neither Donna nor Becky attributed the headaches to anything more than strained eyes and too much studying. But just a few days later, while Becky was discharging her duties as dorm supervisor, she collapsed. She was rushed to the hospital, but never regained consciousness.

When we finally arrived at the hospital, the doctors informed us that the headaches Becky had been experiencing were caused by an aneurysm in her brain. They explained this as a bulging, weak spot in the wall of a major artery. Under the pressure of pumping blood, the aneurysm had finally exploded, sending a shock wave and massive bleeding throughout her brain. The one factor for which we could be thankful was that it would have been instantaneous, causing her no pain.

> The doctors informed us that the headaches Becky had been experiencing were caused by an aneurysm in her brain.

For the next seven days, Donna and I remained at Becky's bedside. Now we would have given anything for just a little of the constant wakefulness she'd displayed as an infant. The hospital provided a bunk that Donna and I used in turn, one of us always sitting at Becky's door, in case she recovered consciousness. Unlike hospital regulations today, we weren't allowed to stay inside Becky's room, where she was hooked up to all kinds of machines and doctors and nurses were constantly carrying out various procedures. But there were visiting hours when we could be at her bedside.

It was Donna who showed herself the strongest throughout this crisis, never reverting to hysterics, always maintaining a calm, hopeful front to our sons and to me, though I knew she was feeling as distraught inside as I was. Stephen and Brian were not with us, as Donna's mother had kindly volunteered to take them to her home in Charleston for the duration, though we kept in touch by phone. Neither Donna nor I went home even for a change of clothes, and I can still remember the tweed suit that I wore for the entire duration of our vigil.

Sitting there, watching my precious, unconscious daughter, there were so many things I wanted to say to her. Regrets I've had to face ever since. For one, I hadn't told Becky nearly enough how much I loved her. Some of that is the fault of my own upbringing. My mother and I never had a demonstrative relationship. When I left for the Merchant Marine, ours was not a tearful goodbye. She'd simply given me a punch on my shoulder and said, "Honey, be good."

When we had our own children, Donna and I tried to have a different relationship with them than either set of our parents had had with us. We'd done our best, learning as we went. For my part, as the provider for the home, I made sure all my children had anything they needed and even more if I could.

I remember one such episode in particular. During her teens, Becky had two front teeth that were giving her some sort of trouble for which the dentist had suggested getting caps. Becky was well aware we were short on funds, so when she came home from the dentist, she said to me first thing, "Hey, Dad, look at my teeth! Aren't they beautiful?"

"Yes, they look beautiful," I admitted cautiously, guessing there was a reason she was bringing this up.

"Well, the dentist had two caps for seventy dollars," Becky went on. "But they didn't look as good or natural as these ones, which were ninety dollars. I knew you'd want me to have the best so I chose these."

If I wasn't happy about paying twenty extra dollars we didn't really have, I can give myself credit that I just let it go without saying anything about her extravagance. I am so glad now that I didn't. Those caps still looked beautiful to the end of Becky's life.

But verbally expressing love to my first-born wasn't something that had come easy to me. In fact, only twice can I remember saying the actual words. Once was when Becky was fifteen. I don't remember what the occasion was, but when I told Becky that I loved her, she gave me a big hug. Her reaction did something to my heart. She seemed so joyous, so thankful, just to hear me say those words.

> When I told Becky that I loved her, she gave me a big hug. Her reaction did something to my heart.

The second time had only been six months earlier. I had picked Becky up from the University of Maryland to bring her home for summer vacation. She told me of her plans to visit her boyfriend at Virginia Tech. When I cautioned her about the visit, as any father might, she burst into tears.

"Daddy, don't you trust me?" she wailed.

I was so overwhelmed by her tears that I had to pull the car over. We both had a good cry, and I apologized, emphasizing my love for her. Ever since, I've wished I hadn't said anything about her plans, though my intent was only good. I wished I had shown her that I trusted her unconditionally.

During those seven days in the hospital, Becky never did regain consciousness. I will never forget when the physician, Dr. John Lord, came out to tell Donna and me that there was no hope for Becky's recovery. Donna and I both began to cry. Then I saw that Dr. Lord was weeping as well. I learned at that moment what it meant to know real empathy for those in pain.

On January 24, 1970, our beautiful daughter left us to pass into the presence of her heavenly Father. Donna and I were both completely torn up inside. It was the single most devastating event in our life, far more so than the death of our little daughter Ellen Kay, in part because we had known and loved Becky personally for so many more years. The precious little girl we'd rarely had to raise our voice to, our obedient, self-reliant, smart, funny, caring, beautiful Becky, was gone. It was equally devastating for our sons, who had just lost their older and only sister.

If Becky's death was the worst of the worst for both Donna and me, it also confirmed the best of the best. We were comforted by the absolute assurance that she was with her heavenly Father and that one day we would see her again. Once again, Donna demonstrated her strength. Though as crushed as any mother can be at the loss of a child, she turned to me and quoted one of our favorite verses to comfort me, the same promise Jesus Himself gave His disciples when they were distraught about Him leaving them:

> Let not your heart be troubled; you believe in God, believe also in Me. In My Father's house are many mansions; if it were not so, I would have told you. I go to prepare a place for you. And if I go and prepare a place for you, I will come again and receive you to Myself; that where I am, there you may be also
>
> —John 14:1-3

I remember saying back to Donna as we hugged each other and wept, "All is right with our Becky. She's with our Lord and Savior, and we'll be with her again."

We also reminded each other of those precious promises in the apostle Paul's epistle to the Thessalonians:

> But I do not want you to be ignorant, brethren, concerning those who have fallen asleep, lest you sorrow as others who have no hope. For if we believe that Jesus died and rose again, even so God will bring with Him those who sleep in Jesus. For this we say to you by the word of the Lord, that we who are alive and remain until the coming of the Lord will by no means precede those who are asleep. For the Lord Himself will descend from heaven with a shout, with the voice of an archangel, and with the trumpet of God. And the dead in Christ will rise first. Then we who are alive and remain shall be caught up together with them in the clouds to meet the Lord in the air. And thus we shall always be with the Lord. Therefore comfort one another with these words.
>
> —1 Thessalonians 4:13-18

I don't know what we'd have done if this had happened before we came to know Jesus Christ as our personal Savior and Lord. I don't know if we could have survived the burden of our grief. Perhaps our marriage and family would have just fractured under the weight.

But though we wept and grieved and would never truly heal from the loss of our precious daughter, of Stephen and Brian's dearly-loved sister, we found comfort in the knowledge that our parting was—and still is—only temporary. Becky is waiting for us in one of those mansions Jesus has prepared for His children in glory. Whether we remain alive until our Lord returns to this earth or are called home first, I have no doubt she will be at the very forefront of that great crowd of witnesses, all our family and friends who've gone before us, that will be there to welcome us into God's presence.

Donna and I have been waiting for more than forty-five years for that day. And there is one thing I know for sure now. Our reunion with Becky isn't so far away anymore. And passing through the valley of the shadow of death will never again be a frightening thought to us because our precious daughter as well as our Good Shepherd, Jesus Christ our Lord, will both be waiting for us on the other side.

CHAPTER ELEVEN

PRESSING FORWARD

If in this life only we have hope in Christ, we are of all men the most pitiable. But now Christ is risen from the dead, and has become the firstfruits of those who have fallen asleep.

—1 Corinthians 15:19-20

I t was under extreme emotional stress that I began my new duties. We quickly sold our Baltimore home and moved to Philadelphia. We spent six months there in a temporary rental, during which time we ended up building our own home. We would live in that house for the next forty-two years, the longest either Donna and I had ever put down roots in one place.

As with prior moves, we also found a good, Bible-teaching church to plug into. Donna and I were both active in church activities, and I ended up as chairman of the board of trustees there. Despite our continued grief, Donna and I clung to the hope we had in Christ that Becky was not gone from us, but only gone ahead.

In some ways, it was easier for me than Donna because I was very busy with my new responsibilities and finding them a gratifying challenge. While I had little knowledge of the home heat market when I started, I had a private secretary (called "personal assistant" these days!) and two very experienced senior management personnel who answered directly to me, which was a big help. There were also six district managers and their personnel working under me.

By a year after Becky's death, I had grown into my new job responsibilities enough that the regional vice president called me into his office to ask if I'd take on an additional assignment. Pat Jacob was the manager for Gulf Oil's eastern region with some thirty-five hundred employees working under him. One of the subsidiaries under his oversight, J.J. Skelton, Inc. in Bryn Mawr, PA, had tallied two hundred thousand dollars of deficit the prior year. Would I be willing to add the company to my other responsibilities and see if I could turn it around? If it couldn't be turned to a profit within a year, Gulf Oil would sell it.

I'd never turned down a challenge yet, so of course I said yes. I couldn't neglect my other responsibilities, so I spent only my free hours studying the failing subsidiary and trying to determine what I call the "heartbeat" of the company. Two things came to light within those first two weeks. The first was that I identified one young employee, Peter Troilo, who had clear potential. I promoted him to office manager and had him report directly to me on a daily basis along with giving me a weekly overview.

The other issue was the inefficiency with which J. J. Skelton was handling its home heat deliveries, which came to light just by doing the math, never my strong suit, but clearly even less so for the prior manager! The subsidiary was running twenty-one 3500-gallon trucks, each making at least thirty stops a day, with a total of about six thousand customers. In the home-heat market, we work on what is called the K-factor, which is the ability to predict how much fuel each homeowner will use so that we show up to top off their tanks before anyone runs out. This K-factor varies, of course, depending on how cold temperatures get, the rate at which each customer consumes fuel, and other factors.

Typically, you want to top off the fuel before the tank gets much below one-third full. I discovered the man handling the K-factor was topping off the tanks at 2/3rds full, which meant the trucks were making twice the runs needed. By reducing those runs, I was also able to reduce the needed trucks from twenty-one to just eleven. By the end of the first year, we'd gone from a $200,000 loss to a profit of $120,000. By the fourth years, profits were well over $300,000.

> By the end of the first year, we'd gone from a $200,000 loss to a profit of $120,000. By the fourth years, profits were well over $300,000.

From then on until I retired from Gulf Oil in 1983, J. J. Skelton ran at a profit. If that sounds like I'm tooting my own horn, in reality the subsidiary had been so poorly managed and loosely run by the time I assumed responsibility that it didn't require any unusual management expertise to turn it around!

The other big challenge I faced during this same time period was the 1973 Arab oil embargo. Since WW2, petroleum had been a seller's market, plentiful and cheap so that any half-competent oil company could make a fortune hand over fist, and Gulf Oil was no exception. With the embargo, petroleum products were in such short supply that the federal government began a rationing program, particularly with the major oil companies. To complicate matters for Gulf Oil, Kuwait had nationalized its oil fields, among the biggest in the world, which to this point had made up 50% of Gulf Oil's production. Not only was there now a major oil shortage on a global scale, but also within Gulf Oil.

The regional vice president again called me into his office to inform me that I would be responsible for rationing out the billion-plus gallons of fuel oil produced annually by Gulf Oil. Specifically, my job was to ensure Gulf Oil complied with all government regulations. My signature on every contract would be the guarantee of Gulf Oil's compliance.

This was an assignment for which I'd been made. My advantage was plenty of experience in going broke and of having to run a business effectively on a shoestring. I was able to streamline and increase efficiency so that even with rationing, Gulf Oil was able to maintain a profit. As with past positions, I also made a commitment to treat each customer fairly, impartially, and with integrity.

As result, during the entire rationing program, we didn't receive a single complaint from the government or any of our customers. Once rationing ended, Gulf Oil sales shot up—in part, I believe, because of the reputation we'd built of integrity and fair-dealing. I can honestly say this was not only the biggest challenge I faced, but my most rewarding experience in twenty-eight years with Gulf Oil.

We did have one close call when a Gulf Oil jobber—i.e., a wholesaler who bought product from us to distribute to customers—called, complaining that he'd been refused product at our Allentown, PA, terminal. He'd been a customer of Gulf Oil for thirty-two years, and he figured we had no business refusing him service now.

"I know there is ample product in your tanks!" he informed me irately.

"You're right," I replied. "However, isn't it true you've received every gallon of your rationing allocation?"

"Yes, that's true," he admitted.

"Every gallon of product in those tanks has a jobber's name on it," I went on, "as due them on their unused allocation. Isn't it good to know that Gulf Oil safeguards every customer's entitlement?"

He agreed he didn't want what was not rightfully due him. I then told him, "Listen, for the moment why don't you beg or borrow enough inventory from another jobber to serve your customers the rest of this week. And next week, I'll have available some additional product you can use as payback. Fair enough?"

Needless to say, Gulf Oil had a customer for life. Later at that year's New Jersey Petroleum Jobber Meeting, that same man asked for a moment at the mike, where he gave high praise to Gulf Oil for handling the situation professionally and ethically.

I could say plenty more about my years with Gulf Oil, but enough is enough. I worked hard to do my job well and had high annual performance ratings from the company as those subsidiaries under my oversight continued to make a profit. Not that everything went my way at Gulf Oil. On two occasions, I refused to go along on a superior's order, which cost me to some extent. But integrity was far more important to me than profit or promotion, and my conscience remained clear.

Of course, I was pleased to have my performance rated favorably by the people to whom I reported. But let me just add this. Timing is everything! I was the right person in the right situation with Gulf Oil. In the 1940s and 1950s, Gulf Oil was making a profit before the product ever reached the pump. They didn't need to worry about profit on our end, only volume. With the Arab oil embargo and Kuwait nationalizing its oil fields, the playing field leveled, and we had to focus on selling the product.

> Timing is everything!

I wasn't that good at sales by nature, but I learned to be good at it. Had I been born at any other time in history, I might not have come out so well. I don't care who you are, timing is important. People are dealt a hand, more or less fortunate, and timing comes in.

All that said, it wasn't my timing since I didn't really do anything except walk through doors as they opened in front of me. The timing was God's, and I will always be so thankful to God for giving me these opportunities, which by any human standard should never have come my way.

In 1983, by which point I'd been working for Gulf Oil twenty-eight years, I was offered a special early retirement deal, which involved one year's pay and a non-discounted retirement. At this time, Gulf Oil was in the process of merging with Standard Oil of California (SOCAL). Once that merger went through, the company was rebranded as

Chevron throughout the United States. I'd been offered the chance to move to the "new" Chevron Oil Company's regional office in Baltimore, but I turned it down.

Not that I planned to just retire and sit around. I was only fifty-seven years old, and I had plenty of energy and drive still in me. Instead, I had my sights on another venture, which was to once again form my own company, not in coal mining this time, but petroleum sales. My objective for Alpine Petroleum Company, as I named my new venture, was a combination of transporting number two fuel oil as well as selling number two fuel oil to jobbers, both those I knew from past contacts and, hopefully, new clients as well.

Of course, this meant competing against major refiners in the area. Reasonable people just might question the wisdom of this action.

CHAPTER TWELVE

RISKS AND REWARDS

For which of you, intending to build a tower, does not sit down first and count the cost, whether he has enough to finish it?

—Luke 14:28

W hen I formed Alpine Petroleum Company, I told Donna we were going to buy product from the major oil companies, take some of their customers away, sell that same oil to those customers, and make a profit. That didn't make sense to her. But it made perfect sense to me. I had our plan for success all worked out, and in my mind, we couldn't fail.

With Gulf Oil dissolving into Chevron, that left a lot of their long-term employees scrambling for work. I was able to hire three former Gulf Oil employees—two salesmen and one very capable office supervisor—with decades of work experience. Donna became company accountant, assuming the vital responsibility of accounts payable and accounts receivable. Not that her salary in the beginning was anything more than a promise. We closed in our back porch to serve as company office.

To get started, our final imperative need was a few sizeable lines of credit. I appealed to my contacts, and the result was beyond what I'd hoped. While at Gulf Oil, I had established an excellent working relationship with Fred Haab, owner of the F.C. Haab Petroleum Company, and Wallace Leventhall, president and majority owner of Royal Petroleum Company, both of which companies distributed petroleum in our area. For more than fifteen years, Gulf Oil had profited from those relationships and so had Fred and Wallace. So they were both willing to offer Alpine Petroleum a line of credit that between the two of them totaled almost a million dollars.

What was more unusual was that neither man asked for collateral, a financial report, or even a written agreement, but were willing to go for it just on my word and a handshake. That is what comes from building a reputation of trustworthiness and that your word is your bond. And though it didn't turn out to be so easy, I proved myself worthy of their trust. Over the following nine years, I never failed on any commitment to them, and both men made a solid profit on their transactions with Alpine Petroleum.

> Your word is your bond. And though it didn't turn out to be so easy, I proved myself worthy of their trust.

In those early days, Alpine Petroleum Company grew by leaps and bounds. We added trucks until we had eight large eighteen-wheel transports, each hauling seven to eight thousand gallons of fuel oil or gasoline. We spread into West

Virginia as well as Pennsylvania and at our height were handling twenty-five million gallons of petroleum products annually. Two key components to our success were purchasing used eighteen-wheelers instead of new and hiring an outstanding diesel mechanic to keep our trucks on the road. The latter I found in Frank Cochran, who could both drive a truck and take care of our mechanical needs.

I can't say enough about Frank Cochran's role in our success. He only had a fifth-grade education, but when it came to keeping our trucks on the road, he was a whiz. Often, he would work a shift as a driver, then stay on for the night shift as our only mechanic. Occasionally, I would quiz him on the condition of each of our eight trucks, eighteen wheels apiece, with specifics about tires and brakes. He could clearly recall all 144 of those items by memory.

> When it came to keeping our trucks on the road, he was a whiz.

Frank was a valuable employee, but our policy as a company was to not be takers only. When Frank bought a small house in New Jersey, Alpine Petroleum made the down payment. Frank also had diabetes that worsened over the years he worked for me. He was treated at a major hospital in New Jersey and, due to medical negligence, lost most of his eyesight so that he had to stop driving. His circumstances didn't sit well with me.

"This isn't right!" I said to Frank. "I think I can help."

With his permission, I put Frank in contact with a lawyer. The lawyer helped Frank settle with the hospital for a sizeable payout. Frank remained housebound, although there was some hope for an operation on his eyes, and he held on to the possibility of working again. When I was visiting him one day, he asked me, "Mr. Kerwood, if I regain my eyesight, would you put me back in a truck for Alpine?"

"Frank, you regain your eyesight, and you'll be in a new truck immediately!" I responded. And I meant it. Unfortunately, he never did regain his sight. People like Frank were the backbone of Alpine Petroleum.

Another factor that made Alpine Petroleum a success was that we were committed to a customer-first policy. If a customer felt we'd taken advantage or failed to deliver in any way, we guaranteed a prompt and fair resolution. In nine years of operation and thousands of transactions, we had only five complaints that I recall. Two were legitimate, and we issued refunds. One was unjustified, but for good will we paid it. The final two were mistakes in billing, which we gladly corrected.

I didn't blame Donna one bit for those latter two. She was raising our sons, being a homemaker, and handling Alpine Petroleum's accounting for very little salary (and originally none!), while her unreasonable husband—me—issued an edict to always send out forty or so invoices a day. It's a wonder she didn't tell us to take the job and shove it, as the old song goes. Her performance and commitment were remarkable and contributed greatly to our success.

I had the same policy in dealing with our employees. Compensation to our drivers was thirty percent of the trucking revenue. With such a small company, I personally kept a record of each driver's daily loads to ensure that any unavoidable delays they experienced were noted and that they were compensated for any extra work hours.

Of course, success doesn't come without some close calls. After Alpine Petroleum had been in business for about two years, I had an opportunity to pick up some new customers in New Jersey, but we had no convenient supply location there. At that time, I was chairman of the board of trustees at my church. The chairman of the deacons was a man named Larry Boykin. He also happened to be the credit manager for Mobil Oil Company, which maintained a refinery in New Jersey. I approached Larry for a credit line so I could purchase product from their refinery to service my New Jersey customers. As manager, he was required to take a credit report, and I offered to put up my house for collateral.

> Success doesn't come without some close calls.

"Ray, I don't want to do that," Larry responded, "I have the authority to approve a credit limit of up to $100,000, so let's go with that."

Larry signed off on the agreement without any collateral at all. If I'd been less than honest, this could have worked out poorly for him, and six months later, it nearly did! One weekend I told a couple of my drivers to pick up loads at the New Jersey terminal to the full extent allowed by our credit limit. The drivers did as I instructed.

The following Monday morning, Larry called me in a panic. Their terminal had not cut off the Alpine Petroleum trucks when they reached our credit limit. We owed $268,000—well over our limit. To complicate matters, two of Mobil's home office auditors were scheduled to start an audit that very afternoon. Larry was beside himself as he could be fired if the error came to light.

Alpine Petroleum had the funds in the bank, so I told Larry, "Look, I know you're on the second floor of your building on Swedesford Road, just a half-mile down the road from me. When we hang up the phone, you head down to the lobby and stop at the Coke machine. By the time you've finished your Coke, I'll be there with the money."

I then asked Donna to make up a check for the necessary funds, got in the car, and delivered the check to Larry as promised. I've often wondered what would have happened if I'd let my brother in Christ down after he'd put himself on the line for me. What a sad day that would have been!

Another time, we found ourselves in a heap of trouble over some substandard heating oil. A refinery in New Jersey had some fuel oil at a good price, so Alpine Petroleum bought a sizeable quantity. From that, we supplied Fred Haab's fuel tanks in Doylestown with about four hundred thousand gallons. Haab's trucks would then deliver the fuel oil to individual homes for heating. We'd only delivered a portion of the order when one of our drivers noticed a waxiness in the fuel oil, a sign that it would congeal in the tanks and ruin the furnaces of any customer's home. Six or seven of Haab's trucks had already delivered the fuel to homes on the previous day.

I told my driver to stop dispensing the fuel. Then I called Fred Haab and told him what was happening. "Fred, I have $300,000 in the bank, and you can have every penny of it."

By this point, I was in a panic. This could be the end of Alpine Petroleum. But Haab wouldn't take my offer. He said he'd work on it. In the meantime, I called the vice president of the refinery from which we'd bought the substandard product. He was aware of the situation. I asked if they'd take back the fuel we'd purchased, then held my breath, waiting for his reply. Legally, I couldn't compel him to take it back. But he agreed to do so and even to split with me the cost of transporting it all back. Over the course of seven days, Haab was able to pull the substandard fuel from their customers' tanks, which was no easy feat. We delivered the substandard fuel back to the refinery, averting disaster with minimal expense and no loss of customers.

> We delivered the substandard fuel back to the refinery, averting disaster with minimal expense and no loss of customers.

Another contract we had with the F.C. Haab Company was to transport diesel fuel contracted from Haab by the Conrail Railroad Company to keep their numerous trains moving. One evening around midnight, I checked with Conrail's dispatcher and was told that no product would be required until 8 a.m. the next morning. Based on this, I dismissed the driver from that shift.

About 3 a.m., I received a frantic call. Two trains would be shut down and stranded unless we delivered two loads of fuel oil by 4 a.m. I called one of our drivers, but couldn't get through on the phone. So I drove forty miles on icy roads in the middle of the night to get him out of bed. We barely made the delivery on time, but the trains were able to maintain their schedule, and we maintained Alpine Petroleum's reputation as being dependable and trustworthy.

I credit Donna with helping me avoid another close call. I was offered an opportunity to close down Alpine Petroleum Company and become a vice president of Amherst Coal Company. The position would have placed me in charge of ten million gallons of petroleum usage annually along with forming the largest petroleum jobber ship in West Virginia, backed by that state's most prominent coal company. Initial projection of profits was in the neighborhood of a million dollars annually.

> I credit Donna with helping me avoid another close call.

I was all for it, but decided to discuss the proposal with Donna before closing the deal. She was strongly against any business proposition that would move us back to West Virginia. Our disagreement was so sharp that, with some embarrassment, I backed out of the tentative agreement. Six months later, Amherst Coal Company sold out to a nationally known company based in Texas, which would very likely have left my family high and dry if I'd taken the position and we'd moved back to West Virginia. Donna is a very observant person, and though it isn't easy for someone like me to admit it when she's right and I'm wrong, I wish now I'd listened to my wife more often.

Of course, business is risky, and if you're unwilling to take controlled risks, you shouldn't go into business for yourself. I've certainly made plenty of mistakes. But the good choices have outnumbered the bad. Let me share one other time a risk paid off, but only because I was aggressive, refusing to give up too soon. In other words, I wouldn't take "no" for an answer.

I'd learned through my younger brother Jim, who still lived in Charleston, WV, that a number of companies in his area were selling a particular product used by coal companies in their sludge ponds that Alpine Petroleum could make available for sale there. Seeing these sale opportunities in my own home state gave me the bright idea to call up one of West Virginia's most prominent multi-millionaires, John Heater. He owned thirty-eight Go-Marts—a combination service station, restaurant, and grocery—across West Virginia.

To supply these locations, Mr. Heater had established a large barge terminal at St. Albans, WV. Mr. Heater was also a majority owner and president of the Bank of Gassaway. So I called Mr. Heater up with a request. Would he be willing to enter into a contract with Alpine for storage and transport of gasoline and diesel fuel?

Mr. Heater promptly and abruptly replied, "Mr. Kerwood, while I've met you once and know of your good reputation, why on earth would you think I'd have any interest in your offer when I've already turned down that same request from Exxon, Pure Oil, Ashland Oil, and Elk Refining Company?"

Instead of taking the hint, I chose to act like he was my buddy. "John, your office is on my way to Charleston. I only need five minutes of your time."

"No," he said.

I refused to give up. "John, I have an approach that I promise you will find beneficial."

"I told you no."

In a courteous tone, I persisted. "John, five minutes is all I ask."

"Okay," he finally agreed with reluctance. "But remember one thing, Ray. Five minutes, and your hind end better be gone."

Five minutes was all it took to sign a deal that led to a four-year lucrative partnership. Without being persistent, maybe even a little pushy, in asking John Heater to consider my offer, none of that would have happened.

I mention these various events to emphasize that during my life there have been a number of decisions that have worked out favorably, not through any particular business acumen of my own, nor happenstance, nor pure luck, but by divine intervention and God's blessing. There is a well-known TV financial expert, Dave Thomas, who whenever he is asked, "How are you doing?" always responds, "Better than I deserve!"

I would say the same. My life and my business career have both been better than I deserve, and I give praise to my heavenly Father, to whom belongs all the credit and glory.

Just to give a family update, both of our sons were grown and out of the house by this time. As with Becky, I will admit honestly I never was a particularly demonstrative parent with the boys. Donna fulfilled that role beautifully and has always been a wonderful mother to all our children. Maybe it goes back again to my own upbringing. But I've always figured that my chief responsibility as a parent was to raise my kids to age eighteen, free of any major concerns or legal and social problems, feeling good in their own skin, able to cope in life, honest, hard-working, and responsible. And of course, knowing their parents love them.

If neither Donna nor I would claim to be perfect parents, our Becky reached adulthood with all that and more. And Stephen and Brian have done well too. They both continued their track record as excellent students from high school into college. Stephen entered the booming field of IT technology and began working with Vanguard Investment firm. He married Mary Jo, who works in IT technology as well for Johnson & Johnson. They have two sons, Chris and Matt. Brian took after his dad by starting his own business, a lawn maintenance company. His wife Beth is a senior VP with Wells Fargo. They also have two sons, Tyler and Austin.

In all, we enjoyed nine good years of business with Alpine Petroleum. But by 1992, it became apparent we couldn't continue to hold our own in the petroleum business. Under the influence of OPEC (Organization of Petroleum Exporting Countries), an association of oil-rich countries across the Middle East and Africa as well as Venezuela, which had been responsible for the 1973 oil embargo, petroleum prices were fluctuating wildly. Just in the Philadelphia area, we were competing with half a dozen major oil companies. One wrong move, and we could be wiped out. So I chose instead to get out while our money was still good and dissolved the company.

> In all, we enjoyed nine good years of business with Alpine Petroleum. But by 1992, it became apparent we couldn't continue to hold our own in the petroleum business.

That was the end for Alpine Petroleum, but not the end of my business dealings. You might say that I just couldn't keep my hands out of other people's business!

CHAPTER THIRTEEN

HELPING THOSE IN NEED

.**.**.**.**.

Therefore, as we have opportunity, let us do good to
all, especially to those who are of the household of
faith.

—Galatians 6:10

"Ray, you're not a bank!" Donna constantly
reminds me.

Maybe not, but God has blessed us as a couple
and as a family, and we in turn count ourselves privileged to
bless others. The love of money may be the root of all evil,
according to Scripture (1 Timothy 6:10). But money in itself
is actually a wonderful commodity that can be used for our
Lord's work and to help those in need all over this planet.
Donna and I count ourselves privileged as well to work
together with others who have a similar passion for using
their skills and finances to further God's kingdom.

To share how all this came about, let me step back for a
bit of explanation and confession. Back when C. W. and Ruth
Lee first led Donna and me to Christ, the Lees took us to hear
a lot of missionaries sharing about their ministries around
the world, but also their needs. And certainly the church we

attended did its share of preaching on tithing, i.e., giving ten percent of one's income to God.

But Donna and I were just coming out of such tight financial times that we were still nickeling and diming every expense. I can remember how baked beans or some other canned item would come on sale, and we'd buy a ton, eating on it till it was gone. Besides, I'd made my own study of tithing in the Old Testament and came to the conclusion that it was really Israel's form of paying taxes, not something Christians were required to do today. After all, I was already paying plenty of taxes to the government of the United States! I gave my share of offerings to church and missionaries over the years, but I didn't feel it had to be some exact ten percent of our income.

> But Donna and I were just coming out of such tight financial times that we were still nickeling and diming every expense. I can remember how baked beans or some other canned item would come on sale, and we'd buy a ton, eating on it till it was gone.

About the time we dissolved Alpine Petroleum, Donna and I began attending a new church. I haven't mentioned the names of all the churches we've attended over the years, but I'm going to mention this one because it's where our own ministry of helping others really took off. Valley Forge Baptist Temple in the Philadelphia suburbs was founded in the early 1980s through the ministry of Pastor Scott Wendel, who continues as senior pastor there. They have since grown to a good thousand in attendance. Their missions program has also grown to the point that today they support 170 missionaries in different parts of the world.

Once we started attending Valley Forge, we began meeting some real heroes of the faith who weren't just working full-time jobs, but serving God mightily in their free time. Among those who continue to have a deep impact on our lives is Dave Davis. In addition to being the chief financial officer of a large industrial company in Harrisburg, PA, Dave continues to serve at the church —twenty-five years and counting—as song leader, choir director, and Sunday School teacher. During his tenure, he has grown the choir to more than a hundred members.

Then there is Pastor Earl Jessup, a church planter for the Baptist denomination with which Valley Forge is affiliated. After Earl shared his ministry at Valley Forge, I invited him out to dinner and was privileged to listen to him share his passion for founding new, Bible-centered churches. Despite battling very serious cancer, Earl planted 167 churches in fifteen years with only three other team members before he passed away not long ago.

Les Wittle is another Valley Forge member with a very special place in our hearts because he was responsible for getting Donna and me actively involved in ministry ourselves. Les Wittle headed up Cornerstone Prison Ministry, an outreach of Valley Forge, mostly to male inmates, but some female, in Pennsylvania's prison system. To illustrate the scope of his ministry, just during the first six months of 2015 (the last period for which I have statistics), he preached to a combined attendance of over twenty-six hundred male and female prisoners. Of those, two hundred and seventy prayed to receive Jesus Christ as Savior.

Les invited Donna and I to participate in his ministry, and we were eventually put in charge of its finances. Along with supporting the ministry financially ourselves, we were invited by Les to visit the prisons with him. The security protocols alone were enough to make me want to stay on the right side of the law! We'd step through a barred entrance into a secure room. Once the bars slammed down behind us, they'd count us all up, check our I.D., and make sure we were all authorized to be there. Only then would a second set of bars rise so we could pass into the prison, rather like an air lock on a submarine or space ship. Then there was the body pat-down. Since Donna was a woman, she'd have to go off to a separate room to be patted down by a female warden.

But it was worth it. Sometimes we'd have up to four services in one day with two hundred prisoners attending each. Seeing those faces light up with the hope of the Gospel was beautiful. Donna and I also began buying Bibles wholesale for distribution to prisoners. Donna did the actual work of collecting addresses of prisoners who wanted a Bible and mailing one personally to each of them. By now, we had also opened our home for small group Bible studies and would often have missionaries stay with us when they were in town.

It was through the prison ministry that we met Lawrence Lantz. Not as an inmate. He was part of the youth group at Valley Forge and began volunteering with the prison ministry, which is how we got to know him. In time, he became like another son to us. He graduated *cum laude* from Rensselaer Polytechnic Institute with an engineering degree, began working for General Electric, married a wonderful Christian girl, and started a family. By 2001, he was moving up the corporate ladder when he answered God's call to be a missionary in Uganda. He has started two churches there and translated the Bible into at least two commonly-spoken dialects of the people to whom he ministers. All this while battling with long-term Crohn's disease.

I might list countless other Valley Forge members and ministry leaders who have also impacted my life and Donna's, but that could fill an entire encyclopedia. I share these few examples to get back to my prior mention of tithing.

By this time Donna and I were giving to missionaries and other ministries, even taking on monthly pledges for some of them like Earl Jessup, Les Wittle, and Lawrence Lantz. But God was really convicting my heart that in not tithing all these years I'd actually been robbing Him and the work of His kingdom. Donna felt the same way, so the two of us sat down and added up all the income God had provided us and how much tithe we had failed to give. God had blessed us abundantly in the dissolving of Alpine Petroleum, so we had the money available. We took that sum and gave it to the Lord through Valley Forge and their various ministries.

> God was really convicting my heart that in not tithing all these years I'd actually been robbing Him and the work of His kingdom.

It was a wonderful feeling to see God's blessing on our lives now paid forward to bless others. But it didn't stop there. It seemed the more we gave away, the more God returned to us, so that we were able to expand our giving well beyond a tithe. I'd had the privilege of hearing Christian entrepreneur R. G. LeTourneau speak way back when I first started with Christian Business Men's Committee, and I remembered how he'd given away more and more of the wealth God gave him until at the end he was tithing 90% of his income and keeping just 10%. We weren't there yet, but it wasn't long before we were helping support twelve different missionaries along with other ministries.

One of the ways God provided for our ministry giving was through my consulting service. One partnership in particular was a special blessing. Pastor Scott Wendel had recommended to a young man in the congregation, Scott McDevitt, that he come talk to me. Scott was in the process of leaving his employer and forming a new company, Translogistics, along with a partner. Pastor Wendel was concerned that this other partner was not a believer in Jesus Christ and that being "unequally yoked" (2 Corinthians 6:14) with someone who didn't share his Christian values could pose difficulties in the long run.

Scott McDevitt and I sat at his kitchen table in the apartment he was renting and laid out a business plan. I offered to share with Scott my fifty-plus years of experience in business, teaching and advising him in whatever measure he desired, at no charge. Tithing his business profits was part of the agreement.

By the end of our discussion, I'd learned that Scott had no way to finance this start-up, so I asked if he would consider me as an investor. We would form a sub-chapter company, with his ownership (along with his partner's) at sixty percent and mine at forty percent. That way he wouldn't have to go to the bank for operating capital, and I would charge no interest in the beginning. His starting salary would be $300 a week with the goal of matching his previous salary of $900 a week as soon as possible. I would serve as president of the fledgling startup at no salary, with the goal that Scott would take over as president if we proved successful.

We almost weren't! I had figured the most I could afford to lose on this endeavor was $25,000. Our business was barely off the ground and we were already down $10,000 when a nationwide strike shut down almost two dozen major trucking companies.

Before the strike, Scott and I had considered which carrier we wanted to use for our product shipping needs. We met with four or five different ones, and the guy with Carolina Freight liked our approach. He got sold on us, so we went with him. When the trucking companies went on strike, only one carrier in our region didn't strike—Carolina Freight. Twelve companies went on strike, and out of the twelve, we just happened to pick the right one! Again, not coincidence, but providence. We soon recovered that $10,000.

That wasn't the only time we saw God's hand on this business. By three years in, Translogistics had outgrown its premises, so I took the responsibility of negotiating the purchase of a former bank building with close to five thousand square feet of space. The building had been vacant for two years and was rundown, but structurally sound. The listing price was $209,000. I submitted a cash offer of $47,500. The realtor called it a ridiculous offer, saying the vice president of the selling bank would laugh him out of the room.

"Tell him it's not his fault you've gotten hold of a backwards, uninformed, former West Virginia hillbilly and that they can reject the offer if they so choose," I responded.

This exchange happened before lunch. The realtor called me at 4 p.m., saying he couldn't believe it, but my offer had been accepted. He wanted me to come to the office the next morning to sign the agreement of sale.

"Nothing doing," I said. "I'll be there in ten minutes with the check."

> The realtor called me at 4 p.m., saying he couldn't believe it, but my offer had been accepted.

And that's what I did. The next day, the realtor received another offer more than twice mine. He told the interested buyers they were a day late and a dollar short. Truthfully, they were only half a day late. I am well aware that this purchase was not the result of my smarts, good fortune, luck, or happenstance. I am confident that it was God providentially taking care of His own. That building served the company well until September, 2012, when Translogistics moved to even larger quarters.

My agreement with Translogistics held for seven years. In 2001, Scott McDermott and his partner let me know they wanted to buy out my stock and disassociate our business relationship, which we did. They both credited me with mentoring them and displaying management acumen that would continue to benefit them. Translogistics has continued to grow tremendously since then, and my prediction of the company's potential worth has been fully realized under Scott's leadership.

Scott McDermott was just one of many Christian businessmen I consulted with or to whom I've loaned money to jumpstart their companies over the last two decades. Most have been able to turn their companies around and are serving the Lord with their success. A few times, the money loans worked out badly, but for the majority, they have been positive.

More pertinently, the proceeds from those ventures as well as Alpine Petroleum became the seed funding to give to God's kingdom. And as I mentioned earlier, Donna and I discovered together that we just couldn't out-give God. The more we gave, the more we got. The more we got, the more we gave.

I don't share this with any suggestion this is some kind of "prosperity gospel" formula where you empty your bank accounts into the offering plate on the assumption that will guarantee so much financial blessing you'll get rich. Not at all. When we give to God, we'd better be doing it out of a generous and grateful heart, not expecting anything in return. Donna and I just know that God blessed us personally with the financial means to give to His kingdom, and He has called us to be faithful in using that blessing to bless others.

Donna and I are now both in our nineties. We don't know how much time we have left here before our life voyage brings us into home port. But our goal, Donna and I both, is that when we reach that last day here on earth, we want to head home with our hands empty and the last dollar we have left given to God. After all, when we face our Savior, the last thing that we are going to be caring about is how much is left in our bank account. What we *will* care about is how many more people we might have helped with what we had left of the blessings God has given us!

CHAPTER FOURTEEN

REBECCA MINISTRIES

-.♠♠-.♠♠-.♠♠-.♠♠-.

O Death, where is your sting? O Hades, where is
your victory? . . . Thanks be to God, who gives us
the victory through our Lord Jesus Christ.
Therefore, my beloved brethren, be steadfast,
immovable, always abounding in the work of the
Lord, knowing that your labor is not in vain in the
Lord.

—1 Corinthians 15:55-58

By the time a new millennium rolled around, God had
blessed Donna and me so much that we needed to
put our giving on a more organized footing. This led
to the realization of a dream that Donna and I had been
thinking and praying about for many years—the
establishment of a foundation in honor of our daughter
Rebecca Jean Kerwood, its sole purpose to fund missions
outreach around the world.

Remembering Becky

Why a foundation? All my life, I've been a businessman, and I believe in the effectiveness of multiplication when it comes to growing a business—or a ministry. Giving to God's servants who are multiplying God's kingdom through bringing others to Christ, who then in turn bring more people to Christ, is the best return on an investment there is. Doing so through a non-profit foundation enlarges growth potential even more by:

- Ensuring that giving has responsible oversight.
- Allowing like-minded donors to work together with us.
- Providing for ongoing funding even after Donna and I are gone.

On May 20th, 2000, Rebecca Ministries was officially incorporated as a 501c (3) non-profit. Its vision statement:

> To reach out a helping hand to men, women and children of all races, nationalities, and creeds, and to present through its witness the Gospel of Jesus Christ.

As with all the heroes of faith who have impacted my life, it would fill an entire book to list individually all the ministries that have been helped and the souls won to Christ through Rebecca's Ministries since its founding. Among early projects was a van for Les Wittle, to make it possible for him to continue ministry despite a deteriorating physical disability, as well as support for numerous missionaries like Lawrence Lantz, Earl Jessup, and others whose ministries and families we already knew well.

Among such missionaries were Ed and Carole Hembrees, missionaries to Romania. We'd gotten to know them because they were among many missionaries we hosted at our home while attending Valley Forge. Rebecca Ministries was able to contribute twenty percent of the cost to build a church that now holds two hundred Romanian Christians. By our reckoning, that means forty of those Romanian Christians are there through the impact of our sweet daughter Becky.

Another such project that has changed countless lives was the installation of a well in a remote village of West Africa that now permits its inhabitants to have clean water for drinking, bathing, cooking, and crop irrigation. Just the children who are no longer dying from dysentery is a major quality-of-life improvement for that village. And through that outreach, the villagers are also hearing the Gospel of Jesus Christ.

Rebecca Ministries has contributed to Russian pastor Vasily Yudintsev, who spent more than eight years in a Siberian labor camp for preaching, where he ended up leading even more people to Christ than when he was on the outside. Others include Tim Berry in the Philippines, Rev. Randall Stirewalt in Kenya, and Dave Zimmerman in the Sudan.

Then there is Mitch Zajac, who spends an average forty thousand miles a year on the road in prison outreach and other ministry. A former drug user and dealer who served eight prison sentences for various crimes, Mitch came to Christ through a Gospel pamphlet he found in a phone booth. He is now one of the boldest and most fearless evangelists I know, routinely facing physical threats while sharing his faith, including a gun in his face.

"God reached into the lowest pit of muck and mire to rescue me," Mitch shares now. "What He did for me, He wants to do for you, too."

But two major focuses of Rebecca Ministries came about through our final move as a couple and through two more heroes of the faith I am now privileged to count as friends. In 2002, Donna and I sold our Philadelphia home in which we'd lived for over forty years. We moved for one year to Charlotte, N.C., then became part of a church plant in Downingtown, PA, about forty-five minutes from Valley Forge, where we purchased the home in which we currently live. Though we are now too far from Valley Forge to attend church there regularly, we maintain close ties with the church and its ministries.

> Two major focuses of Rebecca Ministries came about through our final move as a couple and through two more heroes of the faith I am now privileged to count as friends.

It was in Downingtown that we met the two Williams, or Bill, as their friends call them. When we moved here, Donna and I needed to find a new family physician. A fellow member of the church plant we were attending recommended his own family doctor, a fine Christian physician named Dr. William Brown. Along with his practice in Thorndale, PA, Dr. Brown goes on medical mission trips two to three times a year, primarily to Brazil. On each trip, he treats 350-plus patients and shares the Gospel. An electrical design engineer, William McNamara has invested considerable time since retiring in 2004 to missions and ministry, including traveling with Dr. Brown to Brazil.

Just one story demonstrates how special these two men have been in my own life. I've already mentioned my consulting practice, helping other Christians start companies or manage their finances through difficult times. I've also mentioned that not all those experiences turned out positively. One in particular became a major source of stress. The crux of the issue was that I had made a large loan to someone. He in turn had taken advantage of my generosity and was using every excuse possible to avoid payment. To make it worse, he claimed to be a Christian ministry leader.

One day, I was on the phone with him, pressing for some payment. Instead of being apologetic or showing any gratitude for the loan itself, he began to lash out at me. I was shocked by his response. The next thing I knew, my vision had gone blank and I couldn't form words. I had just managed to hang up the phone when it immediately rang again. I was able to answer it, and I have no doubt that phone call was God's direct intervention. On the other end of the line was my good friend Bill McNamara, to whom I had not spoken in several weeks.

Bill tells his side of that story: "I don't know the reason I called him, but it was clear that he was incoherent. He couldn't express a single sentence or phrase. I thought, 'This man's in trouble.' So I told Ray I'd call him back."

Bill didn't call me back, but instead called Dr. Brown, whose office is just a couple of miles from my house. Within minutes, Dr. Brown was at my house and was administering emergency aid. It turned out I'd had a stroke. The quick response by these two outstanding brothers in Christ during my time of need had undoubtedly saved me from far greater harm. As with other situations in my life, I know without a shadow of doubt that this was not by chance or happenstance, but by God's mercy.

Through the two Bills, Rebecca Ministries not only began supporting the medical mission trips to Brazil, but the ministry of Maria Gusmao. The in-country organizer of those medical missions trips, Maria is also the Brazilian country director for Bible Centered Ministries, International (www.bcmintl.org). Gusmao and her team of volunteers minister to four thousand children each week in some of the worst slums of Recife, a city of about four million in northeastern Brazil.

Rebecca Ministries' other major focus has been with International Partnership Ministries. I've mentioned that one reason for founding Rebecca Ministries is because I believe in multiplication when investing into God's kingdom. IPM provides support for indigenous missionaries throughout Africa, Asia, Latin America. It takes $100 a month to support a full-time missionary in India, Nepal, and Myanmar. $200 in Sri Lanka, Madagascar, or Zambia. In contrast, a North American missionary family sent to the same country will need at least $5000 a month support. Add to that the years needed to learn the language and local culture to become effective in ministry.

This isn't to discourage the sending out of North American missionaries. Every nation has a responsibility in carrying out the Great Commission, and Rebecca Ministries still supports many missionaries from North America. But by supporting indigenous missionaries, we can multiply many times over the number of missionaries enabled to carry out full-time ministry for the same financial investment as one North American. Not to mention that these indigenous missionaries are already fluent in the language and culturally prepared to reach their own people.

IPM, under the leadership of Kevin Callahan, Matt Barfield, and others, is providing such support now in twenty-eight countries. Rebecca Ministries is currently supporting sixteen IPM missionaries ranging from Argentina, Chile, El Salvador, and Mexico to Ivory Coast, Liberia, Kenya, India, Nepal, and China.

To date, Rebecca Ministries has contributed more than a million dollars to global missions, with a current average of about $70,000 a year in designated monthly support to specific ministries as well as one-time donations of up to $250,000.

> To date, Rebecca Ministries has contributed more than a million dollars to global missions.

Meantime, Donna and I are well aware we aren't so young anymore. Just a few months ago, I experienced a health crisis involving congestive heart failure compounded by blood clots in the lungs. When I left the hospital, the cardiologist told me, "You know, you'll never get better than you are right now."

Soon after, I reviewed my records with my own physician, Dr. William Brown. He told me, "From these charts, I don't blame the specialist for saying that. But I don't agree. You are going to get better. I'm going to see you get better."

And he did. Only several months later when I was feeling well again did Dr. Brown very kindly let me know just how close to heaven's gates I'd been and what a miracle it is that I am still alive today. I share that story to show what kind of a compassionate, godly man and outstanding physician Dr. Brown is. But also it made me very aware that Donna and I could no longer handle Rebecca Ministries on our own.

The time has come to pass on the baton. And I am so deeply thankful to the two Bills, Dr. William Brown and William McNamara, who have not only shouldered the responsibilities of heading up a board for Rebecca Ministries, but have now accepted the baton of carrying forward my daughter's foundation, whatever happens to Donna and me.

As I relinquish that baton, giving thanks to the capable leadership God has provided to continue Rebecca Ministries, I think back over the years to our little girl and how from her early childhood she loved to share the good news of Jesus Christ with others. Through Rebecca Ministries, she has played a part in sharing that good news with countless thousands and will continue to do so for many years to come.

One day not so far from now, Donna and I will both be able to share with our sweet Becky all that God has done and the impact her life has had on so many since we saw her last face to face. And together with Becky, we in turn will have the privilege of waiting and watching as, one by one, those who have come to Christ through Rebecca Ministries step through heaven's gates, and we can introduce them personally to the daughter whose life and death helped pave the way for their own journey to the feet of our Lord and Savior Jesus Christ.

Epilogue

Home Port

> Then they cry out to the Lord in their trouble, and
> He brings them out of their distresses. He calms the
> storm, so that its waves are still . . . He guides them
> to their desired haven.
>
> —Psalm 107:28-30

It's now been three-quarters of a century since I stood in as helmsman of that ship coming into Jacksonville harbor and basked in the praise of the port captain telling me, "Well done, young man." At that time, it seemed my entire life was before me, and if I thought about the future, it was with the assurance that I could conquer the world.

Of course, I had no idea then just what kind of crosscurrents life would throw at me. God would use many of those crosscurrents to direct my path. Satan would do his best to use others in an effort to steer me off course. I know now that even when I was such a green, untested, over-confident young man, I was never left abandoned to steer my own course into disaster. Just as on that day in Jacksonville harbor, I've always had a Port Captain watching out for me, directing each step I would take, piloting me through the crosscurrents.

Donna and Ray

That Port Captain is, of course, my Lord and Savior Jesus Christ. Despite my own failings and misjudgments—and there have been plenty—He has faithfully guided me through this life, steering me back on course when I've tried to go my own way. When Satan's intentions were to put me on a collision course with disaster, my Port Captain has taken the helm, guiding me through dangerous waters.

Three-quarters of a century later, I find myself reflecting back over all those decades. The calm waters and stormy billows through which my life voyage has taken me. The days that were sunny and sweet and the icy hurricanes I didn't think I'd survive. Not to mention all those crosscurrents, pleasant and treacherous, through which my Savior has safely brought me.

When I stood at that deck wheel as a young man, priding myself in being the helmsman of that ship, I had no idea just how fast life would fleet by. Now I understand better the words of the apostle James when he queried:

> For what is your life? It is even a vapor that appears
> for a little time and then vanishes away.
>
> —James 4:14

It's gone fast, but believe me, I'm not wishing I was back there, a young man with my life ahead of me. Instead, I find myself longing for home port and to hear from my heavenly Port Captain, *"Well done, good and faithful servant."* (Matthew 25:21).

I am an ordinary man, and I've never thought of myself as anything else. I serve an extraordinary God. And I've been privileged to witness this extraordinary God doing extraordinary things in and through my ordinary life and the lives of so many others.

> I am an ordinary man, and I've never thought of myself as anything else. I serve an extraordinary God.

Dear friend and reader, whether you are barely setting out on your own life voyage with a whole lot of crosscurrents yet to come, or like me you are nearing the end of your trip, I trust and pray that you too have a Port Captain leading you, protecting you, guiding you, and eventually steering you safely into home port. May I finish with a few questions that may help you be certain you are on the right course?

Have you opened your heart to Christ?

Jesus invites each one of us:

> Behold, I stand at the door and knock. If anyone hears My voice and opens the door, I will come in to him and dine with him, and he with Me
>
> —Revelations 3:20

Are you allowing Jesus Christ to be your Port Captain?

One of the most well-known psalms reminds us too have a Guide willing to pilot us to safety in the midst of dangers:

Yea, though I walk through the valley of the shadow
of death, I will fear no evil; For You are with me;
Your rod and Your staff, they comfort me.

—Psalm 23:4

As you voyage through the crosscurrents of life, are you allowing your course to be directed by your Port Captain?

We can fight His guidance, like trying to steer a tanker
through a cross current with hands gripped on the wheel. Or
we can trust His ways and let the current take us on a path
we could not imagine. Psalms 37:23 reminds us:

The steps of a good man are ordered by the Lord,
And He delights in his way.

—Psalm 37:23

Are you confident that when you reach the end of your life, you will find yourself safely in home port, hearing your Savior say, *"Well done, good and faithful servant"* (Matthew 25:21)?

The apostle Paul, sitting in a prison cell and looking
forward to his own eminent homegoing at the hands of a
cruel tyrant, Nero, sums up his own yearning for home port
and his assurance of a warm welcome home:

> I have fought the good fight, I have finished the race, I have kept the faith. Finally, there is laid up for me the crown of righteousness, which the Lord, the righteous Judge, will give to me on that Day, and not to me only but also to all who have loved His appearing
>
> —2 Timothy 4:7-8

I would never put myself it the same category of this great missionary apostle. I'm guessing you wouldn't either. But Paul's words should be an aspiration for all of us. My own hope and prayer as my life voyage draws near home port is that I may finish the race well, having fought the good fight and kept the faith as steadfastly as I can. I look forward to stepping into the presence of my Port Captain, my Lord, the righteous Judge of all the earth, and spending my eternity with all who also love our Lord and Savior Jesus Christ. I'm counting on seeing you there.

Let me finish back where I started. We have an extraordinary God. A God who is faithful, loving, and good. A God who does extraordinary things through ordinary people. I pray that as you've finished reading my life story, that's what you've come away with. Not what a great guy Ray Kerwood is. Nor even what an interesting story this turned out to be. But what a great, good, faithful, extraordinary God you've had opportunity to meet in these pages.

May He guide you safely into home port.